UNDER STARTER'S ORDERS

By the same Authors

OVER THE STICKS

The Sport of National Hunt Racing

UNDER STARTER'S ORDERS

A Guide to Racing on the Flat

Michael Ayres and Gary Newbon

DAVID & CHARLES

NEWTON ABBOT LONDON

NORTH POMFRET (VT) VANCOUVER

ISBN 0 7153 6338 7

Library of Congress Catalog Card Number 74–20465

Set in 11pt on 13pt Linotype Plantin and printed in
Great Britain by Latimer Trend & Company Ltd Plymouth
for David & Charles (Holdings) Limited
South Devon House Newton Abbot Devon

Published in the United States of America
by David & Charles Inc
North Pomfret Vermont 05053 USA

Published in Canada
by Douglas David & Charles Limited
132 Philip Avenue North Vancouver BC

Contents

List of Illustrations

All photographs with the exception of the Derby photo-finish, supplied by Racecourse Technical Services, are by courtesy of the Racing Information Bureau

The racecourse plans which appear in Chapter 13 and the map showing their location, are reproduced by kind

7

permission of the Tote Racing Annual, *by whom copyright is reserved. The map showing the location of Irish courses is reproduced by kind permission of Stud & Stable Ltd, and the remaining illustrations in the text by kind permission of the Jockey Club*

I

The Magic of the Turf

Traditionally known as the Sport of Kings, racing might more properly nowadays be called the King of Sports, for no sport, with the possible exception of Association football, commands anything like the same following and certainly none is more internationally widespread. From the moment man first tamed the wild horse and made him a domestic animal, it was inevitable that some sort of racing would result. There are accounts of a kind of horse racing in the days of the Ancient Greeks, while the Romans are thought to have introduced the sport to Britain during their occupation of the country in the four centuries after the birth of Christ. Chester has records of Shrove Tuesday races dating back to medieval times, while Smithfield, now a famous London meat market, was the venue for races on public holidays during the reign of King Henry II in the twelfth century. The true foundations of the modern industry we know today, however, were laid in the seventeenth century, when the patronage of the Stuart kings gave a great impetus to thoroughbred development, and at the same time established Newmarket as the headquarters of the sport in this country.

Today, racing is a vast industry as well as a sport. Bloodstock exports play a leading role on the credit side of Britain's balance of payments, while the annual betting turnover runs at something like £1,200,000,000, raising a vast sum in tax for the Inland Revenue. Although the betting turnover is usually lower elsewhere (in France, for example, it is only £900,000,000) racing is nowadays a fairly considerable revenue earner in almost every

9

country which encourages it. Even in Holland, a comparatively minor racing nation, the Ministry of Agriculture owns the principal course at the Hague, and does very nicely out of its 2½ per cent share of the Tote turnover. As for general interest, while racing in Britain has suffered, along with other basically spectator sports, from a general falling off in attendances since the boom period of the late forties and early fifties, figures like the betting turnover already quoted, and the estimated viewing figures of more than six million for the Saturday television coverage of racing by the BBC's Grandstand and ITV's World of Sport programmes, speak for themselves.

Great strides forward have been made by British racing in the past ten to fifteen years. Bright young trainers have come to the fore, bringing with them modern ideas and techniques and providing a badly needed stimulus to a branch of the sport that had been in dire danger of becoming moribund. Owners like TV rentals tycoon Mr David Robinson have shown that business-style efficiency can be applied to the buying, training and running of horses, with highly successful results. Security has been tightened up to the extent that 'nobbling'—despite what many a betting-shop punter who has just backed a loser will claim—is now practically impossible, and petty crime, the scourge of racing in the years following the end of World War II, is now virtually non-existent. Technical aids ranging from highly sophisticated video-tape and timing equipment to efficient ways of watering the course are now available, although still shame-fully resisted by some local stewards and officials. In five short years—thanks largely to finance supplied by the Horserace Betting Levy Board—we have seen the introduction, long over-due, of starting stalls, photo-finish equipment on every flat-racing course, better and faster dope-testing, patrol cameras to help stewards ensure fair play, betting shops on the course, syndicate ownership and even lady jockeys—the latter something that would have seemed incredible a decade ago, when even a highly skilled woman trainer had to resort to the subterfuge of applying for her licence in the name of her head lad.

But this sudden rush of progress only underlines how static

and complacent British racing had become. Between Admiral Rous, who rescued the sport from the clutches of the crooks, villains and thieves who virtually controlled it in the early and middle 1800s, and Lord Wigg, who, together with Major-General Sir Randle Feilden, forced the Jockey Club to recognise that racing was no longer a private sport but a public industry, lies almost a century of stupor and neglect. And the blame for this sorry state of affairs is not entirely the Jockey Club's. The forces of reaction are still powerful in the all-important breeding section of the industry, among trainers, officials and even the racing press.

Almost every major innovation for the benefit of the punters who provide so much of racing's income nowadays has been bitterly resisted by the old brigade of trainers. They opposed the introduction of compulsory overnight declaration of runners which ended the scourge of the 25–1 winner that had been a 'non-runner' in the morning paper. They opposed the introduction of starting stalls, standard on the continent for years, which are the only means of ensuring the even break that is the only fair way of starting, particularly in five and six furlong sprints. They opposed the overnight declaration of blinkers—'it's an excuse the stewards cannot argue with when they inquire into a sudden improvement in form, old boy' was the comment of one trainer who shall remain anonymous. And many are still resisting—successfully at the time of writing—the compulsory overnight declaration of jockeys, which again is standard practice in the United States and on the continent. All these measures, it was claimed, infringed on a trainer's freedom. Freedom to do what, one is tempted to ask?

Probably because a racing correspondent, on a big national paper at any rate, works largely away from the office in the company of others doing a similar job for rival publications, racing journalists tend to be a breed apart. Racing is such a time-consuming involvement that they tend to know little, and often care less about other sports, let alone the world outside. In most cases, a soccer or rugby writer will happily switch to cricket, tennis or boxing at a moment's notice, but many racing specialists would find it difficult to compose one hundred words about anything outside their own sphere.

This may explain to some extent why the racing press has so often been a silent accomplice to the turf's traditional resistance to change. Trainers must be 'kept in with' because often they are the only source of reliable information about the well-being of tomorrow's nap selection. Stewards and officials are often highly sensitive to criticism, and can make life distinctly unpleasant for those who incur their displeasure. Jockeys can be touchy, too. In one memorable case not so long ago a top rider took a newspaper to court for reporting, accurately, that he had been booed by spectators after a race.

Racing nowadays is of great importance to newspapers, who often time massive circulation drives to coincide with the start of the flat season, when public interest is usually at its peak. Happy then is the sports editor whose racing correspondent is in a winning run, for a reputation for winner-finding will bring any newspaper a considerable extra following from punters, and a resulting boost in sales. Especially important is the fate of the correspondent's nap selection. This is the one he considers to be the best bet of the day. It may not be the most certain winner (as if there were ever such a thing) because the obvious 'nap' may be all too obvious, and therefore likely to start at too low a price to be worthwhile as a betting proposition. Avoiding these hotpots can, however, sometimes backfire on the journalist concerned, for occasionally a horse that is generally regarded as a good thing, and consequently passed over, 'takes a walk' in the betting when it comes to the race itself and wins at 3–1 or 4–1 instead of the anticipated odds-on.

The record of most newspaper correspondents' nap selections is detailed in one or both of the sporting dailies, the *Sporting Life* and the *Sporting Chronicle*, which feature tables showing the profit or loss to a mythical £1 win bet on each day's nap, and award substantial cash prizes for the expert who ends each season with the highest profit. The *Sporting Chronicle* table is by far the more competitive of the two, featuring as it does over seventy correspondents from national and provincial daily and evening papers as well as Sunday publications and specialist racing weeklies. The *Sporting Chronicle* also publishes each correspondent's nap, and in many cases his full selections for all meetings that day, on the morning of the races. The *Sporting Life*, on the other hand, confines its competition to morning papers only, although a few provincial ones are included among them.

But while selections, and especially naps, are important for sales, most editors realise the immense interest, too, in news stories concerning the sport. Of course none can match the in-depth coverage of the specialist racing dailies, but most of the national papers have a man on the course whose primary function is to report on the racing scene and its personalities, both two-legged and four. Men like Peter O'Sullevan, of the *Daily Express*, Jim Stanford of the *Daily Mail* and Claude Duval, of *The Sun*, regularly bring their readers exclusive stories of new developments, or changes in plans affecting big races in the near future, while every provincial paper is provided with a detailed coverage by staff men of the Press Association news agency who attend every meeting. The agency also issues lists of runners and riders, four-day declarations and betting forecasts to newspapers, and even makes selections for each day's races for those papers without a correspondent of their own. The Press Association 'naps', incidentally, appear in both the *Sporting Life* and *Sporting Chronicle* tables under the nom-de-plume of 'Argus' of the *Liverpool Post*.

For sheer literary style, John Oaksey, who rides as an amateur with great success under National Hunt rules, and is also a most entertaining host on ITV's World of Sport most weekends, is probably racing's answer to cricket's Neville Cardus and Geoffrey Green on soccer. His *Sunday Telegraph* column on the day after Brigadier Gerard's final race in October 1972, was a fitting tribute to a champion:

Back on the scene of his greatest triumph Brigadier Gerard said a memorable goodbye at Newmarket yesterday.
A huge crowd came to watch him win the Champion Stakes

and, for the seventeenth time in three magnificent years and eighteen races, he did them proud.

Even the English weather—to blame in the past for some of the Brigadier's most hair-raising exploits—did its duty. His bay coat glittered in the sunshine and, on the dry, fast ground he loves, the question of failure never arose.

I don't know exactly where Joe Mercer planned to take the lead but The Brigadier made up his mind three furlongs out. Sweeping gaily passed Steel Pulse, he stormed away and, as the commentator called his name, a delighted roar rolled across the Rowley Mile to make him welcome.

Riverman, bravely answering prolonged and extreme pressure, ran on to take a respectful second place and Lord David was third, four lengths away. But they were just the courtiers—the King was safely on his throne.

Men, women and children raced and jostled for places to see him return and the hedge of photographers barring his way was thick enough to turn a film star green with envy. To most horses the crowded, noisy enclosure would have looked and sounded like a corner of hell but The Brigadier's stride never wavered for an instant.

Ears proudly cocked, he seemed, as always, to love it all, and as Mercer dismounted for the last time a call for three cheers went up—something I have never heard before on any racecourse. Then it was over. Mercer gave his old companion-in-arms a final pat and Laurie Williamson, who has looked after The Brigadier ever since he came to West Ilsley as a yearling, led him away through an honour guard of helmeted police.

No British flat race horse has ever given his public better value or served his grateful owners more faithfully. Heaven knows when we shall find another to take his place and the only thing left to say is thank you.

It is always sad to see a champion depart, and although this book is not about racehorses as such, we feel justified in recalling the Brigadier's going at some length, especially in view of the eloquence of this particular retirement eulogy. For it is horses like Brigadier Gerard, and moments like those described above, that make up the true magic of the turf.

2

The Governors of Racing

There is something very British about a major industry such as racing having as its supreme ruling body a self-electing, self-perpetuating association of amateurs who were originally formed as a kind of exclusive social club with aims no more lofty than to promote good fellowship among racing and horse-breeding gentlemen.

Yet this body, without any legal status whatsoever, has ruled the sport in Britain for over two hundred years. It writes the rules, appoints the officials who see those rules are carried out, registers owners and their horses, licenses trainers, jockeys and even racecourses. It has the power to fine or suspend, or even ban for life, anyone in racing who breaks its rules; the rules which have in the main stood the test of two hundred years and are the model for practically every other national racing body in the world.

It was in 1752 that the Jockey Club, which originally met in London and quickly grew in authority and stature because many of its members happened to be important men of the time, acquired the lease of a plot of land in Newmarket—probably on the site of the present Jockey Club Rooms—and built a coffee room. Its early influence in racing was as a kind of arbitration council to which disputes arising at the various independently organised meetings up and down the country could be referred. In fact, one of the first such cases was of a dispute at an Irish meeting—at the Curragh in 1757. A year later the club issued its first authoritative order, on the subject of overweight, and

eventually drew up its own rules of racing which were imposed
initially only at its own meetings, but which gradually became
accepted, along with the club's supreme authority, as governing
all official racing in the British Isles.

Before the Jockey Club's rule was accepted, racing was a
hotbed of crime, corruption and violence. Doping was rife,
jockeys, stewards and judges were regularly bribed, and more
than one clerk of the course absconded with the prize money.
Such offences as ringing, rough riding and bumping and boring
were commonplace. All this, the Jockey Club cleaned up.

Today, the members of the Jockey Club include half a dozen
dukes, among them Prince Philip, four or five earls, various
other aristocrats, a number of bankers, brewers, and builders
and a fair sprinkling of high-ranking military gentlemen, but no
women. Women never have been allowed to become members
and, given the continuation of the club in anything like its
present form, it seems unlikely that they ever will be. Altogether
there are some ninety members, but the real power is vested
in the nine stewards, headed by the triumvirate of the senior
steward, at present Lord Leverhulme, and his two deputies.
These and the other six stewards are delegated to four main areas
of control: licensing; public relations; administration and finance
and discipline. (See Fig 1, p 21.)

The supreme power of the Jockey Club has waned a little in
the past decade because of racing's growing dependence on
funds supplied by the Horserace Betting Levy Board, an official
body established by Act of Parliament in 1961 and headed by
a government-appointed chairman. The board is responsible for
assessing and collecting a levy from bookmakers and the Tote
amounting to more than £7 million each year and is charged
with the duty of applying the money so raised to three main
objectives: the improvement of breeds of horses, the advance-
ment and encouragement of veterinary science or education, and
the improvement of horse racing. Three members of the Levy
Board are appointed by the Jockey Club, three more, including
the chairman, by the Home Secretary (the Act stipulates that
these other two must be persons with no interests connected

Page 17 Racing's 'Corridors of Power': inside the Jockey Club Rooms at Newmarket

Page 18 A trainer's yard: horses at Nigel Angus's stables near Ayr return from the gallops to find a stable companion enjoying a roll on the grass

with horse-racing). The chairman of the Bookmakers' Committee and the chairman of the Horserace Totalisator Board also serve as ex-officio members.

For five momentous years, until the end of 1972, the chairman of the Levy Board was Lord Wigg, a racing-mad ex-colonel who had been Paymaster-General in Harold Wilson's first Labour Government. Unlike his predecessor, Lord Wigg was not content merely to organise the levy (running at something like £5,000,000 by the time he left office) and then hand over the money for the Jockey Club to allocate as it saw fit. Wigg insisted on having the last word in the destination of every single penny of the funds, and the result was a series of conflicts which at first had a beneficial effect on the sport, for if nothing else they brought home to the more recalcitrant members of the Jockey Club, who may not have been entirely aware of the fact, that the twentieth century was not simply with us, but already half over. In fact, after a few initial squalls, Lord Wigg achieved a remarkable affinity with the then senior steward of the Jockey Club, Major-General Sir Randle Feilden, and between them these two men from vastly different backgrounds, the one a shrewd politician and the other a talented administrator, pushed through the most far-reaching series of improvements and reforms racing had known since the 1850s.

It is all the more to be regretted, therefore, that in the closing stages of their joint reign, the old bitterness seemed to return. Whoever was to blame, the result may well be the hastening of a statutory British Racing Authority to assume full control and end the division of responsibility at the top. The idea of a new super-authority was first put forward in the Benson Report on the future of racing, published in 1968, and the Jockey Club have stated that they would welcome its setting up. The authority, which would have a government-appointed chairman, would take over the functions of both the Levy Board and the Tote. Only a lack of parliamentary time would seem to be delaying its formation.

The new authority would allow the Jockey Club to concentrate on its principal function, as rule-maker and disciplinary body,

B

although there would be set up a court of appeal against decisions made by the stewards of the Jockey Club. In addition, the authority would represent the interests of the Racecourse Association and bookmakers. Another body which would probably find itself absorbed into the new set-up is the Joint Racing Board, at present the policy-making body of the industry. The senior steward and his two deputies represent the Jockey Club on the Joint Racing Board, with the chairman and two government-appointed members from the Levy Board. There are also quarterly meetings of a body known as the Joint Associations Liaison Committee, which includes representatives of the Racecourse Association, owners, trainers, breeders and jockeys.

Ever since 1773 a member of the Weatherby family has held the position of secretary to the Jockey Club, and although there was a slight readjustment of roles in 1973, when the firm of Weatherby's became part of the newly formed Jockey Club secretariat, the record remains intact, for the present secretary is Mr Simon Weatherby. The famous family name first became linked with racing in 1770 when James Weatherby, son of a Northumberland solicitor, was appointed Keeper of the Match Book. Today, the firm acts as the civil service of racing, operating both from a London office suite in the Portman Square building which also houses the Jockey Club and Racecourse Association, and from a sparkling new computerised centre at Welling-borough, Northants.

Here different departments keep the accounts of 11,119 registered owners, handle the complicated paper work involved with entries (415,000 in 1973 alone) handicapping, four-day declarations, withdrawals from future events, and overnight declarations; register horses (there were around 15,000 in training early in 1974) owners, trainers, jockeys and colours; control horses' names; publish the *Racing Calendar*, the Jockey Club's official weekly journal, and maintain the General Stud Book on which the whole of the thoroughbred breeding industry depends.

In addition, they print racecards for most of Britain's race-courses; publish detailed records of stallions, mares and their

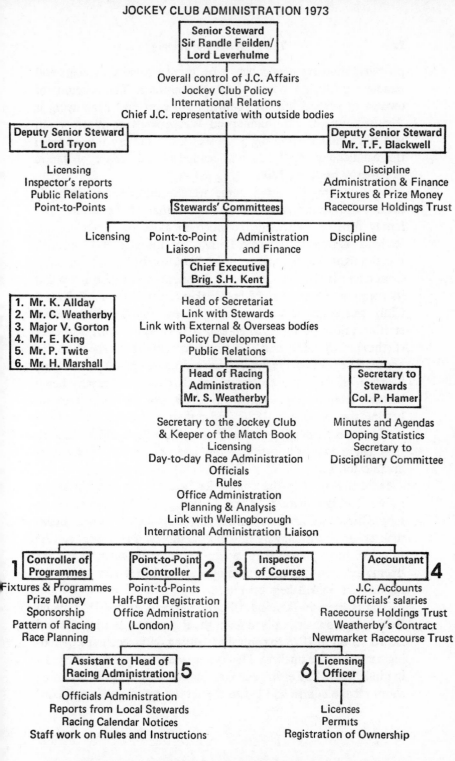

JOCKEY CLUB ADMINISTRATION 1973

Senior Steward
Sir Randle Feilden/
Lord Leverhulme

Overall control of J.C. Affairs
Jockey Club Policy
International Relations
Chief J.C. representative with outside bodies

Deputy Senior Steward
Lord Tryon

Licensing
Inspector's reports
Public Relations
Point-to-Points

Deputy Senior Steward
Mr. T.F. Blackwell

Discipline
Administration & Finance
Fixtures & Prize Money
Racecourse Holdings Trust

Stewards' Committees

Licensing   Point-to-Point   Administration   Discipline
             Liaison   and Finance

Chief Executive
Brig. S.H. Kent

1. Mr. K. Allday
2. Mr. C. Weatherby
3. Major V. Gorton
4. Mr. E. King
5. Mr. P. Twite
6. Mr. H. Marshall

Head of Secretariat
Link with Stewards
Link with External & Overseas bodies
Policy Development
Public Relations

Head of Racing
Administration
Mr. S. Weatherby

Secretary to the Jockey Club
& Keeper of the Match Book
Licensing
Day-to-day Race Administration
Officials
Rules
Office Administration
Planning & Analysis
Link with Wellingborough
International Administration Liaison

Secretary to
Stewards
Col. P. Hamer

Minutes and Agendas
Doping Statistics
Secretary to
Disciplinary Committee

1 Controller of
Programmes

Fixtures & Programmes
Prize Money
Sponsorship
Pattern of Racing
Race Planning

Point-to-Point
Controller 2

Point-to-Points
Half-Bred Registration
Office Administration
(London)

3 Inspector
of Courses

Accountant 4

J.C. Accounts
Officials' salaries
Racecourse Holdings Trust
Weatherby's Contract
Newmarket Racecourse Trust

Assistant to Head of
Racing Administration 5

Officials Administration
Reports from Local Stewards
Racing Calendar Notices
Staff work on Rules and Instructions

6 Licensing
Officer

Licenses
Permits
Registration of Ownership

Fig 1   The Jockey Club chain of command: this administration system
was introduced early in 1973

progeny, showing how much prize money they have won; and handle a growing amount of foreign business. The accounts of owners in several foreign countries are kept and dealt with at Wellingborough. The high-speed Weatherby's computer room and ultra-modern printing processes are a far cry indeed from the candlelight, quill pen and leather-bound ledger of James Weatherby back in 1770.

Another time-honoured name which still plays a vital role behind the scenes in British racing is that of Tattersall. The family firm of Tattersalls, founded in 1766 by Yorkshireman Richard Tattersall, is world famous for the sale of bloodstock but the name survives, too, in the world of betting. Tattersalls' Committee is the betting world's supreme arbitration body and its membership consists of bookmakers, members of the Jockey Club, and some of the journalists responsible for determining starting prices on the racecourses. It is backed by the authority of the Jockey Club and can report defaulters to the club for appropriate action, including the ultimate penalty of being 'warned off Newmarket Heath' which effectively means being banned from racing. Tattersalls drew up the first rules on betting transactions in 1886, and although revisions have been made to meet changing circumstances since then, the framework they laid down still provides the basis on which bookmakers operate today.

Incidentally, it is the connection with the betting industry, rather than that with racehorse breeding, which has resulted in most British racecourses having a Tattersalls enclosure. Bookmakers are not allowed in the members' enclosure so the principal firms station their agents on the rails which divide the 'members' from the main betting ring, or Tattersalls, where the major cash bookmakers operate.

The Horserace Totalisator Board, which operates the Tote on British racecourses, evolved from the Racecourse Betting Control Board set up in 1928 to control all betting on racecourses, including that with bookmakers. This system was changed with the passing in 1961 of the Betting and Gaming Act which legalised betting shops off the course and led to the setting up of the Levy Board to ensure some financial return to racing from the bookmakers who derived their living from the sport. Further legislation in 1973 enabled the Tote, which already had a nationwide credit service, to offer its clients, both cash and credit, the option of betting at starting price, as with a bookmaker, in addition to the traditional pool type bets. The 'machine' as it is referred to by most bookmakers, can also accept bets on other things beside racing now, and can issue ante-post lists and bet on major races abroad such as the Prix de L'Arc de Triomphe and the big Irish races which attract a number of British runners. But the Horse-race Totalisator Board, like the Levy Board, is a government-sponsored body, run by a chairman and three 'directors' all appointed by, and answerable to, the Home Secretary.

In Britain, betting on racing, both on and off the course, is 'taxed' in two often confused but quite distinct ways. Racing's share comes from the levy determined each year by the Horse-race Betting Levy Board, and based on the turnover handled by each bookmaker. The latest levy scheme, that for the financial year 1975–6, is expected to yield £8 million. The amount a bookmaker pays ranges from a flat-rate minimum of £25 for the firm whose annual turnover does not exceed £10,000, up to 0·89 per cent of turnover for bookmakers handling more than £10 million during the year, two-thirds of which is cash betting. The Tote's contribution is decided by a separate agreement.

Quite different from the levy, both in the manner of its extraction and the purpose for which it is raised, is the betting tax. There was no tax on horse-racing betting until the budget of April 1967, when the rate was fixed at 2·5 per cent. In March 1968 the rate was increased to 5p in the £ on all bets. Two years later, the off-course rate was increased to 6 per cent, but on-course bets continued to be taxed at the old rate. Then, in July 1972, after strong representations from the racing world, the tax on betting on the racecourse was reduced to 4 per cent to encourage racegoing. The latest change, in Mr Denis Healey's March 1974 budget, further increased the differential between on-course and off-course betting. He raised the off-course tax to 7·5 per cent, while the on-course rate remains at 4 per cent.

Strictly speaking, the tax is on a punter's stake, but the vast majority of bets are made on the basis of tax deductions from winnings plus stake, on winning bets only. Thus, a punter staking £1 and losing will pay no tax (the bookmaker will, of course, have to pay it for him) but if his £1 bet wins, for example, £9, he will have tax at the appropriate rate deducted from both the stake and the winnings. At 8·5 per cent, the rate most betting shops work at to cover their liabilities over both tax and levy, this would mean his return of £10 (£9 winnings plus £1 stake) would be subject to a deduction of 85p, on which the bookmaker would, in fact, pay only 7½p. It should be stated, however, that most leading firms will allow the punter to pay tax only on his stake if he so wishes, provided he stipulates this at the time he places his bet. The rate of deduction, incidentally is far from standardised. It can be as low as 8 per cent, and in Northern Ireland is usually 10 per cent.

Although the betting tax was, naturally, an unwelcome imposition when it was first introduced, the financial wizards of the bigger firms have seized upon a very lucrative sideline resulting from it. Although tax on cash betting, which accounts for the overwhelming majority, is collected at the time from the punter, it is only paid to H. M. Customs and Excise at monthly intervals. A firm with a number of betting shops, therefore, quickly builds up a very sizeable pool of liquid capital which many of them have skilfully used to finance lucrative 'diversifications' into other spheres. It is to a considerable extent the betting tax which has led indirectly to the booming profits currently being declared by the big bookmaking concerns.

The sort of money involved can be seen from the Customs and Excise total receipts from betting tax on horses and greyhounds since the tax was first introduced in 1967. In the first full year, the tax brought in £30,237,000 for government funds. It was estimated that the figure for 1974–5 would be around four times as much.

Figures like these put the £8 million levy contribution of the betting industry to racing itself into perspective. It is ludicrously small in comparison to the £46 million that French racing collects from a very much smaller turnover on their all-Tote system of betting. But there are countries in an even worse position than Britain. Irish Republican betting shops, for example, pour more than £3¼ million into the coffers of the Dublin government each year from a tax on off-course betting of no less than 20 per cent, exactly twice the British rate. And not a single penny of it goes back into Irish racing! The Irish Racing Board, which covers racing in both Eire and Northern Ireland, does, however, receive a considerable revenue from on-course betting. In 1972 this amounted to £1,384,000, the bookmakers contributing £697,000 and the Tote £687,000. It seems a lot, but there would be few owners, trainers or racing administrators in Ireland who would not prefer a system similar to the British one, if not levied in British proportions! It is interesting to note in fact that British racing gets approximately 1 per cent of the turnover on off-course betting, and the government 7·5 per cent. In Eire it is nothing for racing and 15 per cent for the government. In the South African state of Natal, racecourses split a 15 per cent rake-off from betting on their tracks 50–50 with the government and they also collect 5 per cent of the off-course turnover. New York's non profit-making Racing Association, which runs the courses at Belmont Park, Aqueduct and Saratoga, shares a 14 per cent deduction with the state authorities.

Set beside percentages such as these, it is a staggering thought that just 1 per cent more from turnover than its present allocation would double the income of British racing, to something more than £15 million a year, amply enough to solve so many of its pressing problems.

3

Behind the Scenes

In any part of Britain one is never far from a racecourse—and rarely more than a couple of hours' journey from one staging top-class racing—if not continually, like Ascot or Sandown Park, then at least for a few days each year. The geographical spread of the major British courses ranges from Goodwood in the south to Ayr in the north; from Newmarket in the east to Haydock Park in the west; and this range, plus the fact that not one of these thirty-six courses is exactly like any of the others, gives racing in Britain a unique flavour that is the envy of most other countries.

In France all the top-class horses compete on a small circuit of courses clustered within a few miles radius of Paris, with the exception of the August festival at the fashionable seaside resort of Deauville, in Normandy. The American pattern is even more centralised, involving massive fifty- and sixty-day programmes at successive racecourses with horses living, training and racing on the spot. Then, at the end of the 'season', the whole circus packs its bags and moves on to the next port of call.

The ownership of Britain's racecourses is varied too. A handful are still privately owned: the Queen's course, Ascot, and Good-wood, which is part of the Duke of Richmond's estate, being the most obvious examples. The Horserace Betting Levy Board owns three of the major courses near London: Epsom, where the two premier classics, the Derby and the Oaks, are run; Sandown Park and Kempton Park. The Board also has indirect control of Warwick and Nottingham through a limited company known as Racecourse Holdings Trust Ltd, which has taken leases on both courses from the local authorities. The Trust, originally set up to take over Cheltenham, the headquarters of National Hunt racing, is a non profit-making company whose directors receive no fees. Doncaster—home of the oldest classic race, the St Leger—and Yarmouth, are corporation-owned courses; but the rest, the vast majority, are run on a normal commercial basis by private limited companies.

The co-ordinating link between them all is the Racecourse Association, to which all courses must belong. The association acts on their behalf in negotiations with outside bodies such as the BBC and Independent Broadcasting Authority over contracts for television and radio coverage of racing; with the bookmakers' organisations who pay £1 million a year for the race commentaries broadcast in betting shops; and with the Jockey Club itself over any decisions which will affect the day-to-day work or organisation of the courses or their employees. The Racecourse Association is quite independent of the Jockey Club, although the two organisations conveniently share the same building in Portman Square, near London's Marble Arch.

Although, inevitably, they must work in very close conjunction, the division of responsibility between the two organisations is quite distinct: the racecourse management, acting nationally through the Racecourse Association, is responsible for the racecourse itself, its day-to-day running, the upkeep of the track and its buildings; in short, everything, except the actual racing that goes on there. The organisation of this—the kind of races that are staged and everything to do with the way they are run and the people involved, from the officials who give the orders to the lads who look after the horses—is the responsibility of the Jockey Club.

British racecourses that stage flat racing and mixed flat and National Hunt meetings are divided into four groups for the purpose of the Levy Board grants towards prize money. A basic daily grant for each course is fixed according to the group in which it is placed and there are other additional grants for featured or 'Pattern' races; and for meetings on days which are less attractive from the attendance point of view. A course will get no more than its basic daily rate for a bank holiday meeting, for example, but considerably more for a Tuesday afternoon in April or October. The Levy Board also lays down minimum values for races according to the racecourse group.

These values are in two categories: a lower minimum value for maiden races, claiming races, sellers, races for amateur riders or apprentices, and two-year-old races before 1 June. The ordinary minimum applies to all other races on the course during the season. This is how the courses were graded for the 1975 season:

Group One

Ascot, Ayr, Doncaster, Epsom, Goodwood, Haydock Park, Newbury, Newcastle, Newmarket, Sandown Park, York.
Ordinary minimum value: plates £1,400, stakes £1,200. Lower minimum values: plates £700, stakes £600. Basic daily rate, £2,000 per day.

Group Two

Brighton, Chester, Kempton Park, Lingfield Park, Redcar, Ripon.
Ordinary minimum values: plates £1,100, stakes £900. Lower minimum value: plates £600, stakes £500. Basic daily rate, £1,900.

Group Three

Bath, Beverley, Leicester, Liverpool, Nottingham, Pontefract, Salisbury, Thirsk, Windsor, Yarmouth.
Ordinary minimum values: plates £850, stakes £700. Lower minimum values: plates £500, stakes £400. Basic daily rate, £1,100.

Group Four

Carlisle, Catterick, Chepstow, Edinburgh, Folkestone, Hamilton Park, Lanark, Teesside Park, Warwick, Wolverhampton.
Ordinary minimum values: plates £600, stakes £600. Lower minimum values: plates £450, stakes £400. Basic daily rate, £500.

The Levy Board statistics for 1973 show that there were 431 flat racing meetings in Britain (including mixed meetings) at which 29,319 runners competed in 2,784 races, an average of just over ten runners per race. Racecourse attendances at all meetings during the same year totalled 4,426,176, an increase of 5·5 per cent over the previous twelve months, incidentally.

Figures for the contributions to flat race prize money, derived from the same source, show that in 1973 the Levy Board provided just under one-third of the total, £1,413,067 to be precise, with owners contributing £1,292,703 in entry fees and forfeits; racecourses £1,210,436, and sponsors £712,950 out of the total prize money of £4,629,156.

All racecourses have to be licensed, and each meeting sanctioned by the stewards of the Jockey Club. Applications for fixtures are made by the courses and must be accompanied by a statement of accounts for the preceding year, certified by a chartered accountant. A provisional fixture list is then drawn up by the Jockey Club thirteen months in advance and only minor alterations allowed thereafter. The programme of races for each meeting, and the terms and conditions of each event, must be published well in advance in the official Programme Book, and in the *Racing Calendar*, the Jockey Club weekly, and no alteration is normally permitted after such publication.

This programme will usually be the work of the clerk of the course, a local official who acts as the personal representative of the Jockey Club, and is responsible in the final instance for seeing that every aspect of the particular racecourse's activities is carried out in accordance with the rules and any special instructions of the Jockey Club currently in force. Few clerks of the course are at all well-known yet it is the personality and flair of the clerk that sets the tone of any racecourse, and it is no exaggeration to say that he is the most important man in its work.

One of the clerk's most responsible duties is the framing of races; that is, deciding on the exact conditions that will apply to each event in order to attract the largest possible number of runners, the way in which the prize money is to be allocated, and the precise programme of events on the days allotted to the course.

He does not have a completely free hand in devising the conditions of his races. At every meeting advertised in the *Racing Calendar* at least one half of the total amount of guaranteed prize money must be for races of a mile or over for three-year-olds and upwards, and of this sum at least half again must be for races of ten furlongs or more. If they wish, however, courses may choose to calculate these proportions over all their meetings during the season instead of for each one separately, and most in fact do this.

Basically, there are two kinds of race: handicaps and non-handicaps, or conditions races. In a handicap the horses carry different weights, based on their current assessment in the master-list drawn up by the Jockey Club handicappers. The aim is to give each horse an equal chance of winning. A mass dead-heat would be the ideal result; in practice the handicappers regard a photo-finish as an achievement.

Punters are often confused by the fact that horses often also carry different weights in non-handicaps, but here variations are the result of the published conditions of the particular races. Fillies running against colts of the same age, for example, are normally allowed 3lb. In an event not confined to horses that have never won, called maidens, such animals are usually given a weight allowance of between 4lb and 7lb. Sometimes there is a similar concession for horses that have never run. In races open to horses of all ages, younger animals are generally given weight allowances based on the scale of Weight for Age drawn up originally more than a century ago by the famous Admiral Rous, and amended only slightly since. (See Appendix II.) It is in the devising and allotting of the various conditions that the skill of race-framing lies.

The very best horses tend to avoid handicaps, with the exception of the most valuable ones, for the obvious reason that they are inevitably asked to carry very big weights in order to give the poorer horses a chance. Handicap conditions are usually extremely simple, consisting often of nothing more than a fixed penalty in weight, normally 5lb or 7lb, for any entry that has won after the date on which the weights for the race were published.

The 1972 Goodwood Stakes, for example, one of the major handicaps of the big July meeting on the lovely Sussex course, was advertised as follows:

THE GOODWOOD STAKES (HANDICAP) £2,000 added to stakes. For three-year-olds and upwards. About two miles and three furlongs. £4 to enter, £16 extra if declared to run. The second to receive £400, third £200 of the stakes. Lowest weight 7 st 7 lb. Penalties: after July 8th, a winner of a race value £900 . . . 3 lb; or of a race value £2,000 . . . 7 lb.

In fact, there were fifty-four original entries, of which sixteen were declared to run at the four-day declaration stage, and twelve actually did so. Entries therefore, brought in £472 (38 @ £4 and 16 @ £20) to make the total prize-money pool £2,472 and the race was actually worth £1,852 to the winner (excluding his £20 entry fee), £380 to the second and £180 to the third.

The Prince of Wales Stakes, one of the highlights of Royal Ascot's opening day, is a good example of a non-handicap with horses carrying different weights because of the conditions of the event.

In 1972, this ten furlong contest attracted sixty-two entries, including Brigadier Gerard, unbeaten at that time and the winner again here. Thirty-three dropped out at the 'first acceptance' stage; nineteen at the second, and of the ten horses declared to run at the four-day stage, seven actually went to the start. How it was all summarised on the racecard is shown in Fig 2, p 32.

The weights allotted to each horse in a handicap are derived from the current assessment of the horse concerned in the official, computer-stored 'master handicap' which is the work of a panel of six expert handicappers appointed annually by the Jockey Club. One of the six is responsible purely for sprint races, a second for races from a mile to a mile and a quarter; a third for races over more than ten furlongs, and the other three for the traditional 'handicapper's nightmare', the nursery handicaps for

One Mile and a Quarter, for Three Yrs Old and Upwards

3.5 The Prince of Wales Stakes (Group 2)

£10,000 added to stakes
for three yrs old and upwards
ONE MILE AND A QUARTER
£20 to enter,
£20 unless forfeit be declared by .... June 6th
£60 extra if declared to run
The second 20%, third 10%, fourth 3% of the whole stakes
Weights: 3-y-o colts and geldings .... 8st; fillies 7st 11lb
4-y-o colts and geldings .... 9st 2lb; fillies 8st 13lb
5-y-o and up horses and geldings ... 9st 4lb; mares ... 9st 1lb
Penalties, a winner of a Group 2 race 3lb
Or a winner of a Group 1 race 6lb
Maidens allowed 4lb

A   SS 19

62 entries, 33 at £20, 19 at £40 and 10 at £100.—Closed March 22nd, 1972.
VALUES. WINNER £8221.40; SECOND £2384; THIRD £1142; FOURTH £272.60

Fig 2   How a race's conditions appear in the Programmes Book and on the racecard

two-year-olds. Between them, the six compile a series of ratings, from one to a hundred, covering each horse in training, and this master list is revised daily.

Every week the ratings, revised up to and including the previous Wednesday, are fed into the Weatherby's computer and then all that has to be done is for the entries for a given race to be fed in, together with the race conditions, and out come the allotted weights, with each horse's rating converted into stones and pounds, and all adjustments duly made. The system was given an extensive trial in private during the 1972 flat season, and brought into official use in 1973.

Before this, handicappers were appointed to compile weights for particular meetings. They would usually receive the entries about two and a half weeks before the race—often two hundred or more in a single contest—and have to produce their weights within a matter of days. Not unnaturally, dreadful 'clangers' were dropped, and the problem was made worse by the fact that many trainers deliberately entered horses in a fantastic number of events in the hope that they would be leniently treated in one of them, possibly in error. Now, with all weights based on one master handicap, there is no point to this policy, and the result has been a long-overdue reduction in the time between a race closing for entries and actually being run. In Britain, until January 1974 this time lag was at least a month, whereas a fortnight, or even ten days, has been standard on the continent for years. Now, except in the case of big races or classics, entries are made just two weeks in advance in Britain too. Graded racing, which confines a particular race to horses of roughly the same ability range, is another logical development from the centralisation of handicapping and the introduction of the computer. Although well established in many countries, it is still very much in its infancy in Britain, being introduced for the first time for the 1975 season.

The computer's assistance also streamlines the operation of the rule regarding the 'balloting out' of runners in handicaps. The rule is that where there are too many declared runners for the starting stalls or for safety, the required number are eliminated, beginning from the bottom of the weights list. But under the old system there were almost always too many horses jointly on the bottom weight mark and the unfortunate ones had to be decided by ballot. Now, although the minimum weight remains at seven stone, the computer prints out weights below this where justified by the master ratings list, so eliminations can be made on the basis of these figures. Horses left in the race who have been allotted less than seven stone would then carry this weight whatever their original assessment.

When there are too many entries for a non-handicap, the ballot-box is still necessary where the race is sponsored, or where the prize money is more than £1,500. But in other cases the race is split into two or even three parts according to the number of intending runners, and each part carries the prize money advertised for the original event. The only exception is if the number of declared runners is within two of the maximum, in which case the ballot procedure is applied. The Levy Board makes a supplementary grant to courses to cover the additional cost of races that have to be divided.

There are many variations to be played on the basic theme of handicap and non-handicap, and a good clerk of the course will call on any number of them when composing his programmes, in order to cater for as wide a range of horses as possible. With handicaps, for example, he can confine them to a particular age group such as the two-year-old handicaps, called 'nurseries', that are a feature of the second half of the season. Or he can play around with prize money qualifications. A big field can virtually be assured in the later stages of the season by advertising a race catering for three-year-olds and upwards who have not won a race value £1,000 since 1 January of the previous year.

Non-handicap races can have the same sort of rules applied and be confined to particular age groups. They can also, unlike handicaps, be restricted to maidens, and particularly in the early part of the year, most of the lower-value non-handicaps are in fact maiden races of one sort or another.

Selling and claiming races can be either handicaps or not, but in both cases other rules apply. The main feature of a selling race is that immediately after it the winner is put up for auction and sold for a minimum stated in the conditions of the race. This must be at least three-quarters of the prize money or £1,000, whichever is the least. Until 1973, the owner of the winning horse received first prize money, of course, and the advertised sale price of the horse if it was bought by someone else at the auction. But the racecourse took the rest, and on some occasions their profit could be as much as £1,500 or more. So the rules were changed and in such cases now, the original owner receives 10 per cent of any surplus up to £1,000 and 25 per cent of a surplus exceeding £1,000.

Any horse running in a selling race behind the winner may also be 'claimed' by anyone other than the present owner or his wife, but all such claims must be made in writing at least five minutes before the advertised time of the race. If there is more than one claim for the same horse an auction is held, and the racecourse collects 10 per cent of the deal in either event. The minimum price for a claim, incidentally, is arrived at by doubling the prize money and adding £100. So if you like the look of a runner in a £1,000 seller and decide to put in a claim you will need at least £2,100, even if there is no other interested party.

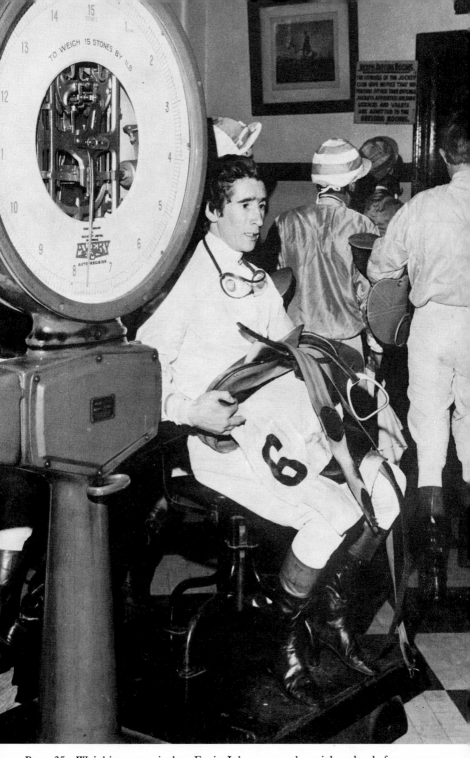

Page 35 Weighing-out: jockey Ernie Johnson on the trial scales before a race

Page 36 Royal Ascot: the ceremonial drive up the course by members of the Royal family is a feature of each day's programme

There is nothing new about sellers. The rules for a race meeting in the Norfolk town of Thetford as long ago as 1669 refer to a selling race whose conditions obliged the owner of 'each horse that starteth' to sell the animal for thirty guineas. But there was no post-race auction as we know it today. The rules continue: 'The contributors present shall throw dice who shall be the purchaser and he who throws most at three throws shall be the purchaser.'

Many owners and trainers dislike selling races intensely, and in 1969 the Jockey Club made an attempt to end them altogether. The minority in favour of their retention, who included the racecourse authorities who see selling races as a welcome boost to their annual income, proved so noisy, however, that they were reprieved, although the original intention of a selling race, to give an owner the opportunity to get rid of a moderate animal, has now been almost forgotten. Nowadays an overwhelming number of selling-race winners are 'bought-in' and even when they are not it is often only because the original owners have been out-bid at the auction. All too often one sees a horse bring off a highly organised betting coup for his connections in a seller, and then be bought in for as much as nine or ten times the advertised selling price. The amount won backing the horse evidently allows for such generosity towards the racecourse concerned.

Sellers probably rank second only to extra-marital sex as the cause of most broken friendships and vendettas in the racing world. But there is no doubt that they often create an 'electric' atmosphere around the sales ring: far more exciting in many cases than the race itself! The record price paid for the winner of a selling race in Britain at the time of writing is 6,800 guineas for a horse called Fair Reward at York in August 1959. No doubt the racecourse authorities, at any rate, considered the name most appropriate.

Claiming races differ from sellers in two ways: the winner is not put up for auction afterwards, and the runners are usually available to be claimed for different amounts. They are allotted weight according to the amount for which their owners are

C

prepared to sell them, so that those with a high 'reserve' carry the maximum and those on offer at lower sums receive allowances in the form of lower weights to carry. As with horses claimed out of sellers, runners cannot be claimed by the husband or wife of the present owner, by the owner himself, or to continue in the same trainer's yard.

Cutting across the basic division of all races into handicaps and non-handicaps is another distinction which is of little or no importance to punters, but which matters a great deal to owners. This is the question of whether a race is advertised as a 'plate', or a 'sweepstakes', which is usually abbreviated in the title to 'stakes'. A detailed explanation of the difference between the two was given on pages 40 and 41 of our book about National Hunt racing, *Over the Sticks*. In a nutshell, the difference is that with a 'stakes' race the money paid by owners in entry fees and forfeits is added to the sum guaranteed by the racecourse and then divided in fixed proportions between the winner, second and third. With a 'plate' the racecourse advertises a fixed sum to be won by first, second and third, with the cash paid by owners being absorbed into the racecourse fund. Naturally enough, owners much prefer the former method! And one can understand their becoming upset by statistics such as those produced by the Racehorse Owners' Association dealing with racing in Britain in 1972. These showed that at Nottingham that year, owners racing their horses in plates had contributed over 57 per cent of the total prize money! The nationwide percentage for sweepstakes, on the other hand, was a much more reasonable 24 per cent.

Although the clerk of the course, in conjunction with the racecourse manager, if there is one, is the man who organises any particular meeting and its programmes, the ultimate authority for the day's racing is vested in the panel of three stewards, local men with a keen interest in and love of the sport. True to racing's amateur traditions, British stewards are unpaid, although they receive professional help and guidance from both the clerk of the course and a gentleman known as a stewards' secretary, appointed by the Jockey Club and allocated by them to each meeting. In theory at any rate, he is a man with vast experience of racing and of the form book, and is expected to draw the attention of the stewards to any blatant form discrepancies shown up by the result of a race or other incidents they might wish to investigate. But he has no actual power himself. He may only advise. Whether the stewards accept his counsel or not is up to them. These stewards' secretaries, incidentally, are sometimes referred to as stipendary stewards, but are in fact nothing of the kind, by virtue of their lack of power. Stipendary stewards do exist abroad and, as the term implies, they have all the authority of British stewards but are professional men; in other words, they are paid for the job they do. In view of the very tricky decisions stewards are often called upon to make, there may be good grounds for believing that at least one true stipendary steward, with the same rights and power as his unpaid colleagues, would be a useful innovation at every British race meeting.

Like magistrates in a lower court of law, stewards at a British race meeting can only impose fines and other punishments up to a certain limit: £50 in the case of a straightforward fine and up to seven days' suspension for an offending jockey. If they feel that any incident warrants more serious consideration or a more severe penalty they will refer the matter to the stewards of the Jockey Club itself. In any case, all inquiries they make, and the decisions taken, are reported to the Jockey Club and are published in the *Racing Calendar*. In the case of jockeys' suspensions, too, the punishment must be confirmed by the Jockey Club stewards within the forty-eight hours before it comes into effect, and the rider concerned has the right to appeal to the highest authority against the decision.

Legal representation is allowed at Jockey Club hearings, both for the man 'on trial' and the stewards, who can impose fines of up to £500 and suspensions for long periods—even for life. But the Jockey Club does not pay legal costs, even if the verdict is 'not guilty'.

As well as the views of the stewards' secretary, local stewards holding an inquiry into a race will also have a report from the ring inspector appointed by Racecourse Security Services on any significant moves in the betting market. Often, although still not often enough, they will have the assistance of the camera patrol film, which provides a record of every inch of the running as well as the all-important head-on view of the finish. The latter can often be a vital factor in deciding the rights or wrongs of an objection in the closing stages of a race. The difference between what appears to have happened from a side-on view of a finish and the same thing seen head-on is frequently startling and it is pleasing to see the camera patrol film of controversial finishes shown more frequently on television nowadays, so that the ordinary racegoer can see for himself the evidence on which a decision has been made.

Other groups of people are working hard behind the scenes to make sure a day at the races is as enjoyable as possible: men like the racecourse farrier, the stable manager, caterers, technical experts and security men. Each of the last two groups are employees of two Levy Board subsidiaries—Racecourse Technical Services and Racecourse Security Services Ltd. They work free of charge to the racecourse. Originally Racecourse Technical Services was concerned only with the photo-finish, but now, twenty-five years after it came into being, it also handles starting stalls, the patrol camera and race timing, in addition to the racecourse commentaries which keep racegoers informed of the progress of each contest over the public address system. One of the company's most successful recent innovations has been the introduction of complete closed-circuit television coverage at some of the bigger meetings, with most of the cost defrayed by commercial sponsors in return for advertising rights.

The racecourse stable manager is always an experienced horseman, and he looks after the welfare of his equine guests with all the concern and efficiency of the manager of a five-star hotel. Whenever he accepts a reservation he will be sure to find out the likes and dislikes of the horse—whether he prefers wood shavings, peat or straw as bedding, for example—and will see to it that everything is done to make him feel at home.

Security of the racecourse stable block is obviously of the

utmost importance. It was formerly contracted out to a national firm, but is now the responsibility of Racecourse Security Services Ltd, formed in 1972 as a result of a special review carried out at the instigation of Lord Wigg and the Levy Board by Chief Superintendent J. E. Watson and Inspector T. Mather of the Lancashire Constabulary. The company co-ordinates the activities of the forensic laboratory which carries out dope tests, and the old security services of the Jockey Club on and off the racecourse. Of the first six directors of the company, three were elected by the Jockey Club, and one each by the Levy Board, the Racecourse Association, and the Horserace Anti-Doping Committee.

Thanks to improvements made over the past decade to security both on the course and off, and the system of random dope testing introduced a few years ago, doping in the old-fashioned manner is no longer the menace it once threatened to become in Britain. The scientists at the forensic laboratory at Newmarket deal with something like three thousand dope test samples a year, but the number found to be positive is remarkably low. In the twelve months between April 1971 and March 1972, for example, samples from 2,270 horses racing in Britain were analysed, and only nine proved positive: all cases involving drugs administered primarily for medicinal purposes, such as the widely used painkiller called phenylbutazolidin, traces of which were found in the urine of Rock Roi after his Ascot Gold Cup victory in 1971.

There have been no takers to date for the £2,000 reward offered by the Jockey Club in April 1972 for information leading to the conviction of anyone trying to dope a racehorse. The offer, made 'until further notice' according to the official announcement in the *Racing Calendar*, came shortly after a controversial statement by Lord Wigg, then chairman of the Betting Levy Board, that 'doping and non-triers' would sound the death-knell of British racing. His lordship's remarks generated a lot of heat at the time, but were never supported by much evidence, at least not on the doping front.

The sensational case of Rock Roi, who was disqualified by the stewards of the Jockey Club and the race awarded to the second horse, Random Shot, did more than anything else to spotlight the immense difficulties of drawing a dividing line between permissible medicaments and non-permissible stimulants in the bewildering array of drugs now available to vets and trainers. 'Bute' as phenylbutazolidin is popularly known, is used principally to help arthritic horses, enabling them to run to their best form, and to give of their best. It could be argued, therefore, that it is not a dope at all, in that it does not artificially boost a horse's performance as would a stimulant, nor cause him to run below par like a depressant. It simply helps him to run without feeling any pain. On the other hand, opponents of its use lay stress on the implications for the future of British bloodstock, always a vital factor when discussing flat racing. If a horse has a weakness, they argue, then he should not be helped by artificial means to overcome it on the racecourse. The initial reputation of a stallion depends largely on his racecourse performance as shown in the form book, and to permit horses to win major races with the aid of drugs to camouflage physical weaknesses would increase the danger of those weaknesses being passed on.

As the rules stand at present, no horse is eligible to run in Britain if he has had 'bute' administered within four days of the race. Other countries are more lenient. In Canada, and some states in America, for example, a horse may run after being treated with the drug provided the fact is declared in advance of the race to the stewards, but the treatment must be continued for the rest of the season. In the case of Rock Roi, the Jockey Club had no option but to take the race away from him, although they obviously sympathised with the dilemma of his trainer, Peter Walwyn, and exonerated him from any implication of malpractice. Rock Roi showed that his 'bute-aided' victory was no fluke, incidentally, by going on to win the Goodwood Cup and Doncaster Cup, beating Random Shot fair and square in the process, but there was another sensation in the 1972 Ascot Gold Cup when Rock Roi again passed the post first and was again disqualified: this time for impeding the second horse, Erimo Hawk, on the run-in. Walwyn, one of Britain's brightest and most successful young trainers, thereby achieved one of the most remarkable 'doubles' of all time; certainly one of the most unwelcome.

Methods of analysis have improved so rapidly in the last few years that traces of drugs or other 'non-normal nutrients' are now being shown up which were completely by-passed before. In the case of Fairzan, disqualified after winning the Timeform Gold Trophy in 1971 because a test proved positive, the offending substance was contained in a vitamin food supplement which his trainer, and many others like him, had been using for years. It was testified at the Jockey Club inquiry that the amount of the substance, theobromine, a drug in the same group as caffeine, found in the horse's urine could have been acquired from a two-ounce bar of chocolate.

In a cogently argued article in the *Sunday Telegraph*, John Oaksey neatly summed up the situation in these words:

> The current rules against doping were designed firstly to discourage dishonesty and cruelty, and secondly to prevent unsound horses establishing on the racecourse reputations which might help them to pass on their unsoundness at stud.
> The first objective does not apply in the cases under discussion, but to achieve the second it is surely only necessary to disqualify a horse if the substance found in him at the time of a race is likely *appreciably* to have affected the result of that race.
> The word 'appreciably' does not appear in the relevant Rules of Racing but at least arguably it ought to. Because if the possible effect of a drug is so small that the result of a particular race could not have been altered by it, then what on earth is the point of disqualifying the winner?

A much more potent long-term threat both to the integrity of racing and the future of the breed is the increasing use on both sides of the Atlantic of steroid-type drugs. Steroids, which have made possible some remarkable advances in human medicine in recent years, are chemical substances normally produced by various glands in the body. Even when synthetically produced in a factory they are virtually indistinguishable from the natural substance and inevitably the problem of detecting their illegal

use in racehorses is a major one. The range of steroids includes
the sex hormones, adrenal hormones and bile acids. Every human
being, and racehorse, has these substances circulating in his body,
and the amount varies from moment to moment according to the
efficiency of the glands concerned, his general health and the
demands of whatever activity is being carried out. Unlike 'bute',
therefore, which is easy to identify as a foreign substance in the
urine or bloodstream, hormones, natural or artificial, will always
be there, and the quantities are very hard for a forensic chemist
to evaluate.

In the United States, steroids fall into the category of drugs
which in most states must not be administered to a horse within
forty-eight hours of racing, but which are otherwise permissible.
Britain, as yet, has no special rule on them, but if their use should
be proved in any particular case there is little doubt that they
would be considered to be 'non-nutrient substances' likely to
affect the running of the horse in question, and consequently
illegal.

It is generally accepted, however, even in official circles, that the
use of certain steroids is going on in Britain. Probably their most
common application is with geldings, whose competitive spirit
can be increased enormously by injections of the male sex
hormone, testosterone. Anabolic steroids, extensively used in
cattle-breeding, can also be very effective as a long-term measure
in building up an animal and developing toughness and stamina,
to say nothing of putting on extra 'condition' which would make
him stand out in a sales ring.

And, like phenylbutazolidin, steroids can be used very effectively indeed as a short-term remedy for soreness, sprains and
lameness. An injection directly into the joint can make a horse
forget his aches and pains and immediately run up to his best
form. The same drugs can cure overnight a 'lame' horse who
would normally take at least a fortnight to get back on to the
racecourse. Any horse who finishes lame and races again within
a fortnight should at least arouse the strongest suspicions of the
stewards.

As long ago as 1972, the president of the Royal College of

Veterinary Surgeons, Alistair Frazer, was quoted by Tim Fitz-george-Parker, himself an ex-trainer, in *The Sun*, as saying:

> There are so many different hormones—such as cortesone, progesterone, testosterone—which have a remarkable effect in conditioning horses fast. Geldings, in particular, can be fantastically improved by testosterone, the hormone they lack because it is produced in the testicles.

From the breeding industry's point of view, the objection to steroids is very much the same as to the purely chemical pain-killers like phenylbutazolidin: their prolonged use may conceal defects which could unknowingly be transmitted to a horse's progeny, and thereby lower the general standard of bloodstock. It has also been suggested that the use of steroids can upset the sexual pattern of colts and fillies retired to stud. Dr William McGhee, a leading veterinary practitioner in the United States, spoke of his experiences in an interview with racing journalist David Hedges published in the monthly magazine *Pacemaker*.

He stated that he had seen a number of horses known to have been subjected to medication during their racing careers which, when they went to stud as stallions, had not come up to normal semen evaluations. Dr McGhee added, however, that it was 'by no means certain that medication was the cause' and, at any rate, given time, these horses had returned to normal and proved perfectly good stallions. In his opinion it was too early to draw definite conclusions from the evidence of what had happened at the American courses where use of steroids is permitted within forty-eight hours of racing, but on the whole he was inclined to favour this method of dealing with the problem by limited control rather than the present British system of outright condemnation, especially in view of the difficulties of detection.

In recent years we have seen the menace of chemical drugs casting its shadow over the Olympic Games and other forms of international sport as well as racing. Scientists claim they can now identify administered steroids in human beings and a concerted effort is being made by equine scientists to achieve the same results with tests on racehorses. Once the breakthrough has been made, it will be up to the racing industry to examine the whole subject of chemical drugs in considerable detail, and arrive, if possible, at an internationally agreed attitude towards them.

Until then it is the short-term use, or rather misuse, of steroids which must give most cause for concern, especially when such use is allied to betting coups which must be little short of outright swindles. The best safeguard of the ordinary punter, and indeed of the honest owner and trainer, too, is unceasing vigilance on the part of the stewards, especially the stipendaries whose job it is to know the formbook. All sudden variations in form must be thoroughly investigated. All too often at present they seem either to pass unnoticed at official level, or to be excused on grounds which, to the outsider, making all due allowance for the unpredictability of equine nature, seem flimsy in the extreme.

4

A Day at the Races

In an age of television and betting shops, many thousands of potential racegoers are content to follow the sport at second-hand. Television presentation of racing has developed to a very high level in Britain, and it is no longer an exaggeration to say that in some instances you can see more for nothing in the comfort of your own home than as a paying customer in the all-too-often crowded discomfort of the racecourse. Close-up views of all stages of the race; instant slow-motion action replays of the finish and other incidents of note; informed comment about the horses and their riders; a constant stream of information on results and betting shows from other meetings; and interviews with various personalities are all part of the service.

But one thing television cannot supply is the atmosphere: that unique mixture of sights, sounds and smells that make up the colourful, exciting, ever-changing panorama of a day at the races. An impartial observer might be forgiven for thinking that the sweltering thousands crammed together into Epsom's grandstand to watch the Derby deserve medals for endurance, but few would swap their coveted places for an armchair view of the same thing on TV. For by being there they are part of the scene, just as essential to the big race atmosphere as the horses themselves or the gipsies on the Heath.

There is obviously something special about the big occasion: the Kentucky Derby, 'Arc de Triomphe' Day at Longchamp, Australia's Melbourne Cup. But the magic of a day at the races can apply equally to more humble events, to Brighton as well

47

as Deauville, Lingfield equally with Longchamp. It is an experience that even non-racing folk should sample at least once.

Two words of advice for the newcomer going for the first time: get to the course early, and go in the principal enclosure. You will need time to get your bearings, because racecourses are complicated places to find your way about—and if you are not in the main enclosure you will miss most of what is going on because it will be happening out of sight.

The two main areas of action at a racecourse are the parade ring, or paddock, and the track itself. Obviously what happens out on the track is of paramount importance, but, particularly at the bigger meetings, watching what goes on in the paddock and in the nearby winner's enclosure, where the first three are brought back after each race to be greeted by their owners and trainers, can be equally fascinating. In fact for some, the sight of the horses for the different races having the finishing touches applied to their preparation in the pre-parade ring provides so absorbing a spectacle that they care little whether they actually see the racing or not.

Realising how spectators love to watch the paddock scene and spot the personalities on view, some racecourse managements are doing their best to make the paddock more easily accessible. When Doncaster was rebuilt a few years ago, the parade ring was re-sited in front of the new grandstand. At Newmarket and Sandown Park cleverly designed balconies enable racegoers in the stand to move a few yards and overlook the paddock. Other courses, unable to go as far as this, make similar concessions to public interest: the enterprising management of York and Redcar, for example, create a temporary parade ring out on the course itself for some of their big races.

In some continental countries the winner's enclosure is incorporated in the parade ring, which can lead to congestion with big fields and short intervals between races, but in Britain it is invariably separate, although usually close by. This enclosure is usually the venue for the auction of the winner of any selling race on the programme, as well as for the presentation of any special trophies associated with a race.

Near the winner's enclosure will be found the weighing room which is, in fact, a series of rooms, including the jockeys' changing room and often the stewards' room and the office of the clerk of the course, as well. In the entrance hall sits the clerk of the scales to weigh the jockeys before the race, and the first four after it, to make sure the weight each horse carries is correct.

Other officials accept the formal declaration of their runners from the trainers, who must also declare their jockey, produce the colours of the horse's owner, and state the weight at which the jockey will ride.

For the professionals, the weighing-room area is the hub of the racecourse activity. Here contacts are made, trainers and jockeys fix future riding arrangements, and report them to the Press Association representative so they can be published in the newspapers. Here, too, other pressmen collect news items and racecourse gossip as well as details about future plans for horses involved in big races in the coming weeks. Watch the weighing-room area at any meeting of consequence and you will quickly spot some of the sport's celebrities as they come and go about their business.

Fortunately, more and more racecourses are realising that they are involved in the entertainment business, and that nowadays this is a family concern. Mother and the kids must be catered for as well as the man of the house. This is especially true of weekend and holiday meetings, where the decision to spend a day at the races may have to be taken in direct competition with the lure of shopping, countryside or a few hours by the sea.

To meet this need, many courses now have a children's playground or playroom where youngsters can safely be left to enjoy themselves on swings and slides, digging in a sandpit or playing on roundabouts, all under the watchful eyes of qualified nursing staff, while mum and dad enjoy their day's racing. At Newcastle, a course with a deserved reputation for hospitality and bright ideas, they have two children's playgrounds. The newer of the two, opened in July 1971, cost £1,000 and features a 'monkey house' with climbing ladders, hoops and trapezes and a climbing frame shaped like an elephant, with the trunk forming a slide.

Other unusual equipment includes a cyclodrome imported from Spain, which children propel in a circle by pedalling; a wall eight feet high with sunken 'footprints' which they can use for climbing it; a look-out tower with a fireman's pole in the middle and an artificial tree for climbing. No wonder youngsters in the Newcastle area are as keen 'racegoers' as their parents.

Another trend which has become most marked in the last decade is the growing preference of the racing public for what might be loosely called 'country courses'. Once upon a time a nearby railway station was a racecourse's biggest asset. It can still be useful, but today a country setting, large, easy-access car parks, and a nearby motorway are very much more so. Former city courses such as Birmingham, Manchester and Alexandra Palace only five miles or so from London's Piccadilly Circus, have been closed down, while once unfashionable tracks like Redcar and Chepstow have gone from strength to strength. Families want to come and enjoy not only a day's racing but a day out in the country as well, and if they are made uncomfortable or overcharged, either for admission or for refreshments, they are quite likely to stay at home and watch on TV next time.

Television coverage is very much a mixed blessing to racing in Britain. The BBC and ITV networks screen as many as ten races on most Saturdays throughout the year, as well as all the principal midweek meetings and several minor ones. There is no question that such coverage keeps people away from the course, especially in bad weather, but there is another side to the picture. Sponsors put up more than £1 million towards the prize money paid in Britain in 1974. Most of it was a direct result of TV coverage of the meetings concerned and the free publicity that would thereby result for their firm's name or products. In addition, the two TV channels pay around half a million pounds direct to the racecourses in fees for the rights to televise their racing. It could well be more, if only the courses would stick together in joint negotiations on fees. Instead, at least two, Newbury and Ascot, have entered into unilateral agreements with the BBC and thereby spoiled the pitch some-what for their fellow members of the Racecourse Association.

Despite high prices, and counter-attractions on television and elsewhere, however, racecourse attendances in Britain have been maintained remarkably well, and even show signs of increasing, at a time when crowds at other spectator sports are almost without exception, going down. And there can be little doubt that increased TV coverage has attracted many people to racing who otherwise would never have dreamed of becoming interested in it.

Having a bet is an important part of the enjoyment for most people at the races, but it is by no means the essential factor that the majority of non-racegoers think it to be. Some even find it impossible to believe that racing journalists, for example, do not back every single one of their selections or, worse, another horse they have been secretly assured will beat it at remunerative odds! In fact, while a few racing journalists do involve themselves actively in the racecourse betting market, helping to place commissions for their stable contacts, the majority simply enjoy a modest wager on their strongest fancies and many of them do not bet at all—either because they feel that to have a financial interest in one of the runners may prevent them giving an objective report of a race or fair comment on any controversy arising from it; or simply because they do not have the time.

The doyen of racing journalists, Quintin Gilbey, in his enchanting autobiography, *Fun was my Living*, relates that after being a keen betting man for most of his life, he gave it up on being appointed 'Kettledrum' of the *Sporting Chronicle* mainly because the demands of his job prevented him from making a close study of the betting market, which, he maintains, is the only way nowadays of making a profit in the long-term.

Racegoers in Britain are more fortunate than those in many other countries in having the choice of both bookmaker and Tote when placing their bets. The difference between the two is not always appreciated by the casual racegoer: briefly, it is that with a bookmaker you strike an individual wager at agreed terms. In other words, £1 on a horse at 3–1 means you must receive £3 plus your £1 stake back (less betting tax) regardless of how much money may have been bet on that horse, or on the others in the race, subsequently. The Tote, on the other hand, works on a pool basis, so the dividend paid out to the holders of winning tickets depends entirely on how big the pool of money invested on that particular race happens to be, and how many winning tickets there are to share it between. But when comparing a Tote dividend with a bookmaker's 'fixed price' return, remember that the former includes the betting tax deduction, which is made along with the other deductions, before the dividend is worked out.

Those who bet in small stakes now have an extra choice with more and more racecourses opening their own betting shops and offering bets at starting price on their own meeting and all the others being run that day. They will even take bets on greyhound races, too, on a quiet day, while the broadcast betting reports and commentaries, just the same as those in the High Street betting shops, keep today's racegoers far better informed than ever they were before.

Course betting shops, like most innovations, were slow to catch on in Britain, but are now spreading rapidly. Even Royal Ascot has one—tucked away in the far corner of the paddock, but well worth the walk. These shops, operated by a national company in which the Levy Board has a stake, are often staffed by off-duty or relief settlers and counter assistants. They will accept all the cross doubles, Yankees and other multiple bets beloved of the British punter, as well as straight bets at stakes as low as 5p on your own meeting and any others taking place on the day. But they do not operate at the racecourse level of betting tax: their normal deduction is the off-course general rate of 8·5 per cent, (8½p in the pound) compared with the racecourse figure of 4 per cent.

So much for where to bet on your fancy, but how to decide which horses to back? The racecard will provide you with basic information such as the names of the horses in each race, together with their numbers and riders' colours to help you to identify them—as shown in the section of a typical racecard reproduced on p 56. But if you want to take a more serious interest in the racing and the form of the runners you need to arm yourself with

Page 53 The inches that decided the destiny of nearly £64,000 of winner's prize money: the official photo-finish print of the 1972 Derby, showing that Roberto (farthest from camera) has just beaten Rheingold. At the top is the mirrored reflection, often invaluable in deciding a result

Page 54 Lester Piggott, regarded by most of racing's professionals as the finest jockey of all time

a copy of one of the two national sporting dailies, the *Sporting Life* or *Sporting Chronicle*. Just about everything you could want to know about the horses on view is contained in their pages but much of the information is necessarily in summary form and those not conversant with all the technical terms of the racing world might find it more rewarding to purchase the special *Timeform* racecard which is produced for almost all British meetings. It is comparatively expensive—80p as against the usual 10p for an ordinary racecard—but contains far more than eight times the information, including a potted history of every horse and its best performances, style of running and current form expressed in everyday language and, almost as valuable, a mathematical rating of each horse's comparative merit. For the novice racegoer there could be no better guide to any day's racing, and even for those with years of experience there is much to be said for the sort of briefing it contains.

The intelligent racegoer also keeps his eyes and ears open for last-minute announcements which can often provide significant clues in the search for a winner. Jockeys, in Great Britain, are declared for their horses only forty-five minutes before the race, so it pays always to check with the number board, or to listen to the names read out over the public address system, in case of important alterations to the riding arrangements published in the morning papers or your racecard.

Overweight is important, too. If it is announced that a horse you fancy is to be ridden by Lester Piggott, or another top jockey, at a pound or two over the allocated weight, you need not worry unduly—indeed it is usually a sign of confidence on the part of the animal's connections. The trainer probably feels this slight disadvantage is more than offset by the benefit to be gained from having a really capable pilot on board, and there is also the point that the weight will be all that of the jockey, and not made up of 'dead weight' lumps of lead in the saddle. If, on the other hand, an average sort of rider puts up more than 3lb or 4lb overweight, this must be a serious disadvantage, especially in a sprint.

Do not forget, either, that the racecourse announcer, when

D

TOTE TREBLE

JACKPOT PREFIX NUMBER 4

One Mile and a Half, for Three Yrs Old and Upwards

3.40 The Warren Stakes

£2000 added to stakes

for three yrs old and upwards that, at closing, have not won a race value more than £1000

ONE MILE AND A HALF

£4 to enter, £16 extra if declared to run

The second to receive £400, third £200 of the stakes

Weights: 3-y-o colts ...... 8st 4lb; fillies and geldings 8st 1lb

4-y-o and up colts ...... 9st 4lb; fillies and geldings 9st 1lb

Penalties, a winner since 2-y-o 3lb

Or, since 2-y-o, of 2 races or of one race value £1000 .... 6lb

Maidens allowed 7lb

A   SS 18

56 entries, 42 at £4 and 14 at £20.—Closed June 28th, 1972.

VALUES. WINNER £1828; SECOND £380; THIRD £180

Form		Trainer	Age	st	lb	Draw
	402 **EXSTREAM**		5	9	10	(2)
2-00120 D	Ch h Exbury—Reel In Major Derek Wigan (K. S. Cundell, Compton) LIGHT BLUE, BLACK cross-belts, RED cap					
	405 **WHITE PRINCE (USA)**		4	8	11	(4)
3000-02	B c White Label—Rajput Princess Mr R. Northedge (G. B. Balding, Weyhill) BLACK and WHITE stripes, BLACK sleeves, RED and WHITE check cap	P. Perkins				
	407 **CHARLOTTE'S PRIDE**		3	8	7	(6)
0140 D	Ch c Charlottesville—Barn Pride Mr W. Parkinson (Major M. B. Pope, Streatley) Mr J. Parkinson BLACK and AMBER qtd, striped sleeves, BLACK and WHITE check cap	P. Eddery				
	411 **TARAMOSS**		3	8	4	(3)
10-2300	Ch c Pardao—Moss Maiden Miss E. B. Rigden (A. M. Budgett, Wantage) CLARET and CHAMPAGNE qtd, CHAMPAGNE sleeves, GREEN cap	B. Taylor				
	413 **COTE D'AZUR**		3	7	11	(1)
30-00	B c Crepello—Monaco Princess Mr Louis Freedman (C. F. N. Murless, Newmarket) YELLOW, BLACK spots, YELLOW sleeves and cap	A. Murray				
	414 **REALGAR (FR)**		3	7	11	(5)
0040	Ch c Right Royal V—Rossellina Marchese Incisa della Rocchetta (J. M. Clayton, Newmarket) WHITE, RED cross-belts and cap	W. Carson				

NUMBER OF DECLARED RUNNERS 6
(STRAIGHT FORECAST)

BLINKERS WILL BE WORN BY NOS. 2 & 5

Average Time: 2 mins. 36.0 Best Time: 2 mins. 35.1

1971: Royalty, 3-8-10, J. Mercer, 13-8 W. Hern 6 ran.

Fig 3 A section of a typical racecard, showing the race, its scheduled
starting time, distance, title and conditions, above a list of declared
runners, together with their form, owner, colouring and breeding,
trainer, owner's colours, age, weight to be carried, and draw for position
at the start. The boxes on the left of the race conditions indicate that
the event forms part of the Tote Treble and is number four in the
Jackpot Six

he is giving information about overweight, will refer to the actual weight due to be carried by a particular horse, and not necessarily the weight figure printed on the racecard. Racegoers are often puzzled by an announcement that goes something like: 'Number eleven 7 stone, carries 7st 2lb', when their card shows the horse as carrying 7st 7lb anyway. The reason is that the announcer is taking the rider's allowance, 7lb in this instance, into consideration. The allowance should reduce the weight carried by the horse in question to 7st, but the apprentice cannot do the weight, so is riding at 2lb over. Again, if he is a young rider of promise, this need not be an insuperable burden. You have to get to know your riders. Serious backers will study the form of the apprentices as closely as the top jockeys and the horses themselves.

The draw can make a considerable difference on some courses, and notes about its effects will be found in the chapter on British Racecourses. More detailed information appears in most form books, or on the programme pages of the two sporting daily papers. In Britain, the horses are always numbered in the draw from left to right as they face the starter, so if you are looking at them head-on from the stands the horse drawn number one will be in the starting stall on the extreme left and the runner with the highest number will be on the far right. The positions are decided by a ballot made at the time the overnight declarations are made, in other words, 11.00am the day before the race in question, and most evening papers and all morning ones will publish the draw, together with the names of any horses wearing blinkers, which must also be declared overnight, in their racecard programme. The introduction of starting stalls to Britain in the middle sixties lessened the effects of the draw on some courses, but it can still be crucial at places like Chester, where horses drawn on the inside of the tight little circular track have to travel a considerably shorter distance than their less fortunate rivals drawn in the higher numbers. Obviously, on any course, the longer the distance of the race the less important the draw becomes.

When the horses arrive at the start they usually circle around

for a while as the starter calls out the names of the jockeys to be
sure that everyone is present and correct. Last-minute adjustments are made to girths that may have worked loose on the way
to the post, and then the handlers begin to load the horses into
the stalls. In the normal way horses drawn with odd numbers go
in first, then the even numbers, but a particularly nervous animal,
or one that is over-excited or reluctant to enter the stalls, may
be put in before the others, or kept to the last at the discretion
of the starter. If a horse is not keen, the assistants will usually try
to help him in by one standing on each side and linking hands
to push from behind. If this does not work, the reluctant animal
is usually blindfolded and more often than not goes in without
further ado. Three unsuccessful attempts are all most starters
will wait for nowadays. If the horse still refuses to enter the
stalls he is usually left behind, and rightly, for the long delay
can upset others who have been cooped up in the cramped stalls
while all the coaxing has been going on.

Once all the horses are installed—or in the case of an 'old-
fashioned' barrier start, once they are all in a correct line
according to the draw—the starter's assistant raises a white flag
and the horses come officially under starter's orders. With stalls,
the signal 'They're off!' usually follows within seconds.

In a special position beside the winning post, the judge will be
waiting to place the first four horses home. Although in Britain
prize money rarely if ever extends beyond third place, he is
required to name a fourth, too, in case a subsequent objection
or inquiry results in any of the first three being disqualified.
The history of the Turf, especially in the early part of the
nineteenth century, is rich with stories of 'bent' judges, whose
view of a finish could be considerably influenced by cash, alcohol
or various forms of hospitality! That sort of thing was happily
brought to an end in the mid-century purges led by Admiral
Rous and others, but a judge's life, even in these well-organised
and mechanised days, can still from time to time prove controversial. Ask punters who backed Brass Farthing to win at
Carlisle on 13 September 1973! After a close finish to the
Champion Apprentice Handicap, judge Gerry Flynn called for

the print of the photo-finish, as he is required to do by Jockey Club rule if the winning margin is less than half a length. Unfortunately, he mistakenly deduced from the print that Brother Somers had won by a head from Brass Farthing, whereas closer inspection later revealed that he had placed them the wrong way round. The stewards gave him permission to correct the result, but since by then it was more than an hour after the race, and the weighed-in signal had been given, the vast majority of bets on the event, including those on the Tote, had been settled, and for betting purposes the original result stood. So the backers of Brother Somers collected their money on an 11–2 'winner' which never won, while the unfortunates whose cash was on Brass Farthing got nothing, even though their horse is in the official records as the winner and his owners have been rightfully credited with the prize money.

With the photo-finish now in almost universal use, controversies over which horse has won are now very rare, and mistakes like the one at Carlisle virtually unheard of. Modern processing methods mean that a negative can be rushed to the judge within a very short space of time and, unless the result is very close, this is usually sufficient for the official to decide the outcome. Only in a very tight finish will he need to call for a print, and even then it can usually be provided within a matter of minutes.

In the early days of the photo-finish camera things did not move so speedily, and a great deal of betting used to take place on how the result would turn out. If an odds-on favourite was involved, and he looked as though he had been beaten, it was often possible to get a better price about him after the race than before! Alec Bird, one of the best-known and most successful professional backers of the post-war era, is thought to have won well over £100,000 betting on the results of photo-finishes after developing a near-infallible technique of his own. He would stand exactly on the finishing line and, completely ignoring the run-up to the finish, simply observe which horse's nose passed over the line first. If it was the one on the near side, he would back it with every pound he could get the bookies to accept, but if it was the one on the far side he would not bet because the one on the far side was almost always the one most people *thought* had won. It was an optical illusion, and it helped Alec to win a fortune before the bookmakers tumbled to his game and began placing their own men on the line to do the self-same thing. Nowadays, with photo results often declared before the horses are back in the unsaddling enclosure, with TV slow-motion replays within seconds of the finish and, worst of all, a 4 per cent tax on both winnings and stake, betting on photo-finishes has virtually died out.

Like the photo-finish, the racecourse commentary is now such an accepted part of the scene that it is hard to realise that it has only been with us since the early 1950s. Test tapes were made at Royal Ascot in 1952 and, as a result, the first public commentary on a British racecourse was organised for the big Goodwood meeting later that summer. The voices heard by racegoers were those of Peter Dimmock, now head of Outside Broadcasts at the BBC, Henry Green, who later became head of the Jockey Club's security section and is now deputy director of Racecourse Security Ltd, and Bob Haynes, who became the first full-time racecourse commentator.

Today every meeting, however minor, has a commentary, given either by a member of the Racecourse Technical Services team of four or five full-timers, or by one of the ten or a dozen part-time men. These part-timers are mostly journalists or reporters employed by the Raceform organisation which produces the official form book and record, so their work keeps them constantly involved in the racing scene. The full-time commentators cover something like one hundred and twenty days racing in a full year, while the others sometimes cover as few as twenty-five days. A team of this size is needed, however, to cope with days such as Easter Monday when there can be fourteen meetings on the flat or over jumps at the same time in Britain.

Some of the RTS commentators also work in television, one example being Raleigh Gilbert, whose chatty but extremely well-informed style quickly attracted the attention of the ITV network, and who makes regular appearances on 'World of Sport'. Peter

O'Sullevan, acknowledged as the finest race-reader in the business and the model for most younger men in his field, also had a spell as a racecourse commentator before establishing himself with fellow *Daily Express* columnist, Clive Graham, and more recently Julian Wilson, as the principal voices behind the BBC's television coverage of racing.

O'Sullevan uses coloured pencils to draw a diagram of each rider's colours alongside the horses listed on the racecard, a laborious task, especially with the big fields that are commonplace in the early and late stages of the season, but one that pays tremendous dividends in the speed with which a particular horse can be identified. Many of the formbook race-readers employ the same technique. But however conscientious your homework, and however good your memory, the sight of thirty or more two-year-olds charging down a broad five furlongs such as Newmarket, for example, is a pretty formidable one, and the skill with which the top men, whether on the course or TV, pick out which is which and who is doing what, is all too often taken for granted by their fortunate listeners.

In a different part of the grandstand another commentary is being given, this time by the Exchange Telegraph team, whose description of the race, and regular reports on the fluctuations of the betting markets, are relayed by private GPO line to their agency's head office in London, and then re-broadcast to betting shops all over the country. Extel, as it is commonly known, is a private company which celebrated its centenary in 1972 with a sponsored race at Leicester. It operated for many years as a news agency providing a comprehensive news and sports results service, principally to newspapers, but since the advent of betting shops has concentrated on its sports service, especially racing, and stock market returns for bookmakers, newspapers and private subscribers. One of their latest developments has been the introduction of televised betting and results information, which is threatening to make the old-fashioned betting shop 'board boys' with their blackboard and chalk a thing of the past in all but the smallest of businesses.

At first you will probably be quite content to let the

commentator sort out the runners and describe the race for you, but as in most other pursuits, there is far more enjoyment to be had from racing by more active participation. With quite a modest pair of binoculars (8×40s would be ideal) and the willingness to memorise a few colours so that you do not have to refer constantly to your racecard, you will quickly find yourself able to follow in detail the running of at least the principal horses in any race—and may well gain the satisfaction of noting a few winners for the future in the process.

Swotting up the colours and committing them to memory may seem like hard work, but it will make your racegoing much more interesting. When people tell you flat racing is boring, it is usually because they are just looking at it as opposed to really watching what is happening. A rugger match can be deadly dull to the spectator who simply sees a bunch of men chasing a ball around a muddy field, but the very same match will often be absolutely fascinating to the connoisseur. It is just the same with racing. Flat racing does not possess the obvious visual appeal of its National Hunt counterpart, but nevertheless it can be tremendous fun for anyone prepared to study the tactical battle going on before his eyes at speeds of up to forty miles an hour.

During the race itself, watch how your horses run, and how they are ridden. In a sprint, the start is obviously all important, especially on a fast downhill five furlongs like Epsom. Note the horse that loses a vital few yards by not being fast enough out of the stalls. Watch how the jockeys ride their race. Some will 'cover the horse up', tucking him in behind the leaders and then try to bring him through with a late challenge. Does it look as though the timing of the challenge was intended, or was the jockey prevented from starting his run because there was no opening? This sort of observation can be very useful in considering a horse's chances next time it runs. Other jockeys will not wait at all, but set out to make all the running. Whether they succeed or not, check on whether these are the usual tactics for the horse concerned. The form book will tell you. Above all, note when the jockey asks the horse for his effort, and what happens. With a good horse the response will be instantaneous.

Even the early stages of a race can prove quite informative as you become increasingly adept at noting which jockeys are sitting quietly with their horses full of running, and those who are having a constant battle with their mounts to keep them up with the others. If a horse is not going well, try to discover the reason. Is it the ground, perhaps? His stride will usually be the clue to whether he is happy with the underfoot conditions or not: a horse who is at home on the prevailing ground will stride out with great zest; one who is not will often race along in short crab-like bounds. Again, the form book is the clue to what going suits a horse best, but your own observations can often be a great help in filling in the gaps for future reference.

Of course, you should pay particular attention to the finish, watching the running of as many horses as you can in the last furlong, not simply the winner and his closest rivals. It is probably worthwhile here repeating the advice we gave in *Over the Sticks.*

A horse who puts his head down and battles on is worth remembering for another day, even if he is beaten this time, and particularly if he is making his first appearance on a racecourse. But beware of the animal who throws his head up, puts his ears back, or swishes his tail. These are usually signs that he does not relish a struggle and is not to be trusted until he proves otherwise.

If you did your pre-racing memorising well you will also be able to spot future winners among the horses which finish in the ruck behind the leaders. The young horse that makes up ground rapidly at the end but does not quite make the frame, may well be just discovering what is expected of him. The horse that is leading most of the way but suddenly runs out of steam in the closing stages, especially if he has not had a race for some time, could also be one to be on next time out. Note your comments on your racecard and check them next morning with the sporting press.

In an exciting finish, or with a big field, it may be impossible to see anything like all that happens. Even the trained observers of the form-book staff generally consult one another after a finish of this nature. If the meeting you are at features closed-circuit TV, you will usually be able to see the action replay of the closing stages again shortly after the race, and this can be very helpful in confirming or disproving your first impressions, as well as showing up things which may have escaped your notice at the time. And the increasingly skilful way you read a race will not only add to the pleasure of your racing but could also pay valuable dividends when weighing up the runners for another race in the future.

5

The Impossible Dream

Sooner or later practically everyone with the slightest degree of interest in racing comes to cherish the dream of one day owning his own horse. For the vast majority, the dream will never be more than just that. But it is with those lucky enough to contemplate turning the dream into reality that the fantastic lure of owning a racehorse is best demonstrated. A century ago much of the flamboyant horse-buying was done by idle aristocrats with more money than sense. Today even business tycoons fully accustomed to examining the smallest detail of an investment before approving it, seem to toss aside all thoughts of caution when confronted with a well-bred yearling which could just possibly win them a race.

The madness is most evident at the annual sales, especially the autumn spending sprees at Newmarket, which caused a writer in the 1972 edition of that august annual volume, *Ruff's Guide to the Turf*, to remark: 'The 1971 Houghton Yearling Sales might have taken place in Wonderland instead of Newmarket, for all the records in the book were demolished, some several times, in the most infectious, devil-may-care spending spree that has ever gone by the name of a yearling sale on this side of the Atlantic. . . . It was patently obvious that only a minute proportion (of yearlings) would ever be worth their purchase price.' The writer is probably still recovering from the shock of finding that the following year's sales set up new records!

Financial journalist Iain Murray, writing in the *Business*

Observer, examined the pros and cons of ownership from the strictly commercial viewpoint, and concluded, not unnaturally: 'If Britain's racehorse owners and breeders have one thing in common, it is limitless optimism coupled with seemingly bottomless pockets.' A baffled Mr Murray quoted facts and figures to justify his conclusion:

> The Racehorse Owners' Association estimates that each racehorse in Britain is maintained in training at an average loss of £1,000 a year, and says that the chances of making the sport pay are minimal. Yet the list of owners reads like a Who's Who of the business world . . . men of proven business acumen who are nevertheless prepared to plough large sums into the outrageously risky world of racing.
>
> Why do they do it? 'Certainly not to make money!' says Sir Jules Thorn, a response that is spiced with a certain measure of irony when it comes from a man who has been at the right end of a remarkable spell of beginner's luck. . . . Sir Edward McAlpine advances an altogether more novel explanation for his racing interests. 'I do it as a counter-irritant to having to be intelligent' he says. 'If I found I was losing too much money, I wouldn't hesitate to get out.'

Without doubting for one moment either the sincerity of Sir Edward McAlpine, or the accuracy of Mr Murray's reporting, the article probably came nearer the heart of the matter in its final paragraph, which quoted property millionaire Mr Louis Freedman's explanation for his becoming 'hooked' on racing. Mr Freedman, who has followed up his original interest by moving into the breeding side of the industry in a big way, buying the Sassoon and Cliveden studs, summed up the magic of owning a racehorse thus: 'The sport of Kings takes on a new dimension. . . . For no one feels more truly a monarch than the man standing in the winners' enclosure waiting for his horse to come down.'

The regal feeling Mr Freedman describes is by no means confined to businessmen. In a few words, he has managed to catch the essence of a magic that has held men of all kinds, kings and carpenters, barons and butchers in its grip through the centuries.

There are countries—Japan being a prime example—where an owner finds it possible to make a reasonable profit from the running of even his more moderate horses from prize money alone. This is either because attendances at the racecourses are extremely high, as in Japan, thus enabling the courses to offer large purses as prizes and still remain solvent, or because the country's system of betting produces a healthy source of revenue for the sport, thus enabling the authorities to heavily subsidise the prizes offered. In France, for example, the prize money for even a modest selling race at a second-class course will be greater than that for many a featured handicap in Britain or Ireland, and this is after all kinds of other facilities have been financed by the colossal (by British standards) rake-off from betting.

In Britain, latest estimates by the Racehorse Owners' Association put the average cost of maintaining a horse in training at more than £3,000 a year, and the average amount of prize money won at £800. So the strictly mathematical odds against any horse paying his way are almost 4–1. And even this figure is probably on the optimistic side when you consider that the prize money totals include the rich pickings from big races like the classics, which are invariably won by a select handful of top-class animals.

But the profit and loss account of a horse's racing career is only one side of the picture, which can often be transformed by taking into consideration the owner's capital investment in the bloodstock business. Most financially successful owners make their money in the sales ring rather than on the racecourse. Even Britain's most consistently successful owner in recent years, Mr David Robinson, whose businesslike approach to the actual racing of his huge Newmarket-based team we shall examine in some detail later on in this chapter, probably does not break even over a number of years on the purely racing side of his operations. But add in the brilliantly successful record of his expert organisation in buying and selling the Robinson horses and there is a vastly different story to tell.

Of course, not every racehorse appreciates in value during its racing days. Even the most promising can turn out to be flops and go down in value. A man with several horses can offset the losses on some of his team by the profits on others, but the man contemplating ownership for the first time will not be in so happy a position. His wisest course will be to make his first purchase a filly, the best-bred one he can find. The reason for this is that there is always a demand for well-bred brood mares, and with world demand for horses increasing all the time, the result can only be an all-round increase in the average capital value. Even a filly who does not manage to win a race, but is reasonably bred and was perhaps placed a couple of times, will almost certainly be worth more at the end of her three-year-old season than she was as an unraced two-year-old. And a victory on her record, however minor, will increase her value even more. Owners of colts can hit the jackpot, too, of course, but there is far less chance of their doing so. A three-year-old colt who has reached October still without a win to his name is unlikely to have much future in the racing world except as a jumper, and will almost certainly be sold, at a loss to his owner.

Back to finance. A prospective owner can expect to pay anything up to £50 a week for training fees alone at Newmarket, although he will still find trainers quoting £20 a week or less in the provinces and in the North. Insuring a £2,000 horse will cost £60 a year at the current average of 3 per cent, and allowing for shoeing and vets' bills, cost of entries and jockeys' fees and other incidentals, a reserve of about another £10–15 a week is advisable. So, assuming as a new owner you opt for one of the £20 trainers, you will still need to set aside something in the region of £2,000 at least as 'running costs' for a year.

There will always be exceptions, of course. Racing would not be the fascinating sport it is without them. Santa Claus, for example, cost eight hundred guineas as a yearling, and went on to win the 1964 Derby. Even more remarkable was the experience of sports commentator Ian Robertson, a former Scottish rugby international, who formed a syndicate with eleven of his rugby friends to buy a two hundred guinea colt which they called Rugby Special. It must have been the cheapest animal trained at Newmarket at the time, certainly the least expensive in trainer Ryan Jarvis's stable, which housed two dozen other two-year-olds which had cost anything from £1,000 to £20,000. Yet Rugby Special, whose owners had chipped in just £20 apiece to buy him, won four of his eleven races and was unplaced in only one of them. He won £3,000 in prize money and the syndicate spent half their profit on a filly that they named Rugby Princess. 'It was an unbelievable dream come true', said Robertson. 'The final irony was when three different people offered us £10,000 to buy our two hundred guinea bargain.'

Such luck is obviously very much the exception rather than the rule, however, and as we have seen, a sum of between £3,500 and £4,000 is the minimum advisable capital required for anyone contemplating ownership in even a modest way. If you are determined to head for the classics first go, you can add a nought or two on to the end of that figure. Even then success would be anything but certain. The great Nijinsky cost the late Mr Charles Engelhard £35,000, a price that was made to look chicken feed when he won more than £130,000 in prize money in Britain alone and was syndicated as a stallion for £2,266,000 little more than two years later. But other rich men and women have spent fortunes in vain attempts to buy, or breed, a classic winner.

Assuming more modest ambitions for your first venture into ownership, therefore, your next move should be to get some expert help and advice. If you know a trainer, have a word with him. He may have a horse in his yard already for you to consider, or know of someone with one to sell that is in your price bracket. Alternatively, you could approach one of the bloodstock agencies, who act on behalf of both buyers and sellers of horses in very much the same way as estate agents do with properties. They make their living by charging a commission from their clients, usually 5 per cent. So if an agency finds your £2,000 dream horse for you they will expect £100 for their trouble. But on the other hand the professional advice of a good agent is invaluable. He can comb the sales catalogues for a likely horse to suit your requirements; provide details of the animal's pedigree stretching back through four or five generations; arrange an independent valuation and veterinary checks as well as actually bidding on your behalf if the purchase is made through the sale ring. This is still the most common place to buy a horse, but by no means the only one. Some breeders, for instance, would rather sell privately, or through a trainer they trust, so that they can be sure of where their young horses are going. In the sales ring, of course, a horse will go to whoever bids the most—provided the sum is more than the 'reserve' figure put on the animal by the seller, in other words the lowest price at which he is prepared to sell.

From the buyer's viewpoint, a strong argument in favour of private sales is the greater opportunity they afford for a thorough veterinary examination. The full drill suggested to veterinary surgeons in a memorandum on examining horses for potential buyers, issued in 1973 by the Veterinary Association, takes over an hour to complete; and this sort of time would rarely be available at an auction.

The memorandum, whose primary purpose was to protect vets from the possible consequences of the Trades Descriptions and Misrepresentations Acts, states that 'all clinical signs of disease, injury or abnormality observed during the examination should be recorded on the certificate'. Most important advice for the inexperienced new buyer is that a warranty covering height, freedom from vices and non-administration of drugs before the sale, or the horse's performance, should be sought from the vendor rather than the vet, since these are matters between buyer and seller and not the vet's responsibility.

But, however you buy, what can you expect to get for your money? Your agent or trainer will obviously be looking for the best possible animal within your price range. With a ceiling of £2,000 it will be no good their looking at classically bred animals, but they should still be able to find a reasonable choice. As a new owner you will probably be keen to see your colours carried to victory as early as possible, so a potential 'early two-year-old' will probably be their suggestion, as well-bred as possible, thinking ahead to a possible re-sale in a couple of year's time.

When it comes to looking at the animal itself, as opposed to studying the sales catalogue, they will be looking for a horse with

Page 71 The Newmarket Sales attract buyers from all parts of the world to the Park Paddocks sales rings of Messrs Tattersall

Page 72 Lady jockeys are comparatively new to the British racing scene. These were the contestants in the Koh-i-Noor Diamond Stakes at Ascot in 1974. The first two champion lady riders, MerielTufnell (1972) and Linda Goodwill (1973) are third from the right and third from the left respectively

a good middle, allowing plenty of room for heart and lungs; strength in both the front shoulders and hindquarters; good bone below the knee, and hocks set right to help his galloping action; wide-set eyes, a sign of honesty and character, and a general air of alertness and intelligence. Provided the young horse is well proportioned, the actual size does not matter anything like so much as some experts would have you believe. The British are obsessed with breeding for size. They ignore the fact that many famous horses of the past were on the small side, and there are very successful ones today who are officially little more than ponies.

It is not always appreciated by owners who are new to racing that their choice of trainer is of vital importance—possibly even more crucial than the actual choice of which horse they buy in the first instance. The situation is not unlike that of an author with a new play. A producer who is in sympathy with his ideas, and who has the talent and facilities to make the most of the material he is given to work with, can perform near-miracles with the most unpromising of scripts. But the opposite is also the case: a poor producer can make a shambles out of Shakespeare. So it is with racing. A Vincent O'Brien, Barry Hills or Peter Walwyn can bring out the best in the most ungenerous animal, while with the wrong kind of handling, even Brigadier Gerard himself might never have progressed beyond lance-corporal status.

The sort of trainer you choose will depend not only on the potential of your horse but the kind of racing you intend to go in for. If you are a betting man, and see your only hope of making ends meet to be landing a gamble every so often, you must obviously find a trainer who places his horses shrewdly and who knows his way around the betting market. There are plenty of them. If, on the other hand, you simply want to run your horse for its own sake, with betting being only of secondary importance, or even none at all, the choice of trainer is equally wide.

There is no harm in getting expert advice on possible trainers —but make sure it is unbiased advice! Possibly nowhere outside the theatrical profession is rumour and innuendo so rife as in

E

racing, and it usually pays to double-check every opinion unless you are thoroughly acquainted with the person expressing it.

Your prospective trainer need not live in a mansion with a half-mile drive and wrought-iron gates—though there is nothing against those that do. There are very good trainers operating in the most unlikely surroundings. But his yard should have a general air of efficiency, and a happy atmosphere. What sort of gallops are available? (Check whether the fees, if public gallops are used, are included in the basic training fee. This could make quite a difference.) How often are they out of action because of hard going? What alternatives are there? How is the staff situation? However good a trainer is, the success of the horses in his care, including your own, will depend largely on the skill, enthusiasm and loyalty of those who work for him.

Your own temperament will also be an important factor in your relationship, and it is essential to establish from the start how you are going to work together. Some trainers will simply tell owners when and where their horses are running and how well they expect them to perform. Others will be happy to let owners suggest possible races. Naturally all owners have particular meetings and races in which they would like to have a runner, but most would have the sense to go along with the trainer's judgement if his advice was that the horse had a much better chance of success elsewhere.

Every prospective new owner must be approved and registered by the Jockey Club on the prescribed form, obtainable on request from Messrs Weatherby. Once accepted he will remain on the list (provided, of course, he does not break the rules and is warned off) permanently, unless there is no return of a horse in training in his name for two consecutive years. No one is allowed to run a horse under an assumed name. After registering himself, a new owner's next task is to register his racing colours on another form from Weatherby's, or provided by the trainer. There are thousands of colour combinations already in use. Some are held by the owners concerned for life, but most are renewed each year at a cost of £2. The choice is by no means completely free. Designs that alter in character when viewed from right to

left—in the back straight and on the run to the post, for example
—may cause confusion in identification and are not allowed in
Britain and most leading racing countries. The best policy is to
decide on which colours, preferably three, you wish to have,
and then work out the detailed pattern with the help of the
Weatherby staff. The range of designs is pretty extensive, from
the usual hoops or stripes, sash or crossbelts to more recent
innovations such as stars, chevrons and the Maltese cross design
featured by Mr Paul Mellon's colours made famous by, among
others, Mill Reef and Run the Gauntlet.

The silks themselves, incidentally, will set you back another
£25 or so, and your spending spree still has not finished. You
will need to deposit £100 with Weatherby's to open your
account, from which entry fees, forfeits and other charges will be
deducted, and into which any prize money your horse may win
you will be paid after the statutory deductions have been made.
These deductions apply in Britain only to first place prize money.
They are 10 per cent for the trainer, 7·5 per cent for the jockey,
4 per cent for the stable staff and an additional quarter per cent
for apprentice training.

One point not always realised is that although the trainer is
the professional side of the partnership, officially it is the owner
who makes the decisions. Entries, forfeits and declarations are
all made in the owner's name and if the trainer is required to
handle that side of things, as most owners will wish him to, he
must hold an Authority to Act from the owner, which costs
another £5 a year. As your agent, the trainer, or anyone else you
care to appoint, can then make entries, declare forfeit, and make
four-day declarations on your behalf. He may also sign partnership forms or lease forms or lodge an objection. But there are
limits : your agent may not sell your horse, for instance, without
obtaining your permission, since this is a matter which falls
outside the rules of racing.

Naming your horse will cost you another fifty pence if he
is a yearling, and £2 or more if he is two years old. All racehorses' ages, incidentally are reckoned from 1 January, irrespective
of the exact date of their foaling. The naming may not prove

as easy as you might imagine. Weatherby's naming department keep a list of all registered names, and regularly publish a list of these, plus other protected names which cannot be used. They include classic winners and horses which have run within the past ten years. Names which are too blatantly advertisements are also supposed not to be allowed, though when one sees the names carried by some horses it is difficult to remain convinced that this rule is regarded very seriously. The name of a horse cannot now be changed after it has reached the age of four.

Entry fees for races range from £2 for the smallest prizes to £200 for the Derby, with more to pay if you declare to run at the four-day declaration stage, and with bigger races, at successive forfeit stages before that. It costs a total of £500 in entry fees to run a horse in the Derby, for instance, whereas you could get a run in an all-aged plate at Beverley for less than a fiver. But as entries have to be made at least three weeks in advance a horse will often be entered in several different races, and even declared at the four-day stage for two or three, but actually run in only one.

A 'passport', or identity card, will be made out for your horse as soon as it enters training. This document, which must always be held by the trainer responsible for the horse, will detail its breeding and markings and will include a diagram picture of the animal from both side and front. The passport must be produced by the trainer as required and is always necessary when a horse goes to race in another country. It must also be produced to the stewards of the meeting at which the horse first runs after returning from abroad, no matter how long has elapsed since his trip. In addition to acting as an identity check, the passport also serves as a useful record of all vaccinations received by an animal.

But the most important feature of the passport system is that it has eliminated to all intents and purposes the practice of 'ringing' —substituting a good horse for an inferior one entered in the same race—which was once rife in the sport. A 'ringer' even won the Derby in 1844 but, thanks largely to the determination and zeal of Lord George Bentinck, the scandal was exposed and

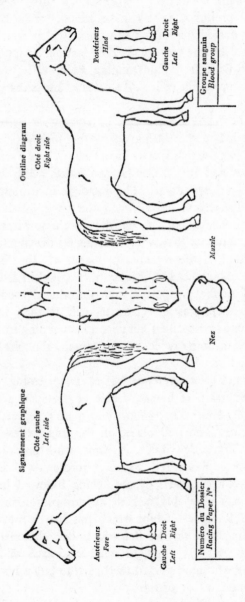

Signalement graphique
Côté gauche
Left side

Antérieurs
Fore

Gauche *Droit*
Left *Right*

Numéro du Dossier
Racing Paper N°

Nez

Muzzle

Outline diagram
Côté droit
Right side

Postérieurs
Hind

Gauche *Droit*
Left *Right*

Groupe sanguin
Blood group

A section of the passport document in which all details and distinctive markings of a horse are recorded when it first comes into training.

the culprits brought to justice. His lordship's efforts were not
entirely without prejudice, it should be added, for he had lost
a great deal of money betting on the horse which was beaten
into second place by the imposter! This 'winner', supposed to
be a three-year-old colt called Running Rein, was proved in
fact to be a four-year-old called Maccabeus, and subsequently
disqualified.

In more recent times, it was a case of 'ringing' at Bath in the
late forties that led to the setting up by the Jockey Club of a
special security force which is now incorporated into Racecourse
Security Services and run jointly by the Jockey Club and the
Horserace Betting Levy Board. The incident in question was
the celebrated Francascal affair, when the gang involved not
only switched the horses but also cut the telephone wires to the
course, so that the money they were investing off the course could
not be transmitted to the racecourse market via the 'blower'.
This is the last known case of deliberate 'ringing' in Britain, a
tribute in itself to the passport system introduced soon afterwards, although there was an accidental mix-up early in 1972
which resulted in a horse called Paradise Lost running in several
races, and indeed winning twice, when everyone thought he was
Hyperion's Curls.

Earlier in this chapter reference was made to leasing, and to
the multiple ownership of horses, a side of the sport which is
developing rapidly and bringing more and more completely new
owners into racing. The trail blazed in the mid-sixties by the
townspeople of Tunbridge Wells, in Kent, who took out five-
shilling shares in their hundreds to run a hurdler to whom they
gave the name of their town, is now being followed in more
sedate, but equally enjoyable fashion by groups ranging from
the semi-official Racegoers Club, which has had a number of
horses in training both on the flat and under National Hunt
rules during the past few years, to small syndicates of friends
or club members who have pooled their cash to buy a horse and
further their common love of the sport.

In addition to syndicates, there are various other kinds of
'special' ownership. Leasing, for example, which operates exactly

as it would with a house or flat, except that 99-year leases are rare! The lessee agrees to 'rent' the horse, and maintain it at his own expense for an agreed period of time, at the end of which it reverts back to the lessor. The terms of the lease are up to the individuals concerned, but must be registered with the Jockey Club and approved by them. Usually the lessee agrees to pay the owner of the horse a percentage of any prize money it wins during the period of the lease, during which time, incidentally, he is himself 'the owner' as far as the rules of racing are concerned, and will be held responsible for payment of bills and in any other matter as though the horse were actually his.

A leasing arrangement is often particularly attractive to breeders. Almost invariably they have young fillies that are potentially useful brood mares, and which they are consequently loath to sell. To put them all into training themselves would be an expensive business but, by leasing, the horses can be maintained at someone else's expense during their racing careers and still be available when needed. Of course, the breeder stands to forfeit a great deal of prize money if the animal concerned is a big success on the course, but in this case she will have become that much more valuable at stud. From the other point of view, leasing can enable a man who could not afford the capital outlay to buy a horse outright to enjoy the pleasures of ownership. He has the fun of seeing the horse run in his name and colours, so is well satisfied by the deal.

A horse owned by more than one person will generally fall into one of the three categories: partnership, club-owned, or syndicate-owned. The exceptions are horses owned by recognised companies which run in the name of a nominee. In all other cases, unlike a leasing arrangement, the members of the partnership, club or syndicate as the case may be, share the actual ownership of the horse. They pay a capital sum towards the purchase price, and they receive a proportion of the eventual sale price, according to their stake in the freehold. With a club-owned horse this will involve the majority of members only very indirectly, since the horse will be bought out of the club funds and the sale price paid back into those funds. But with a partnership or syndicate each member would directly contribute or receive a proportion of the cash according to the size of his or her share in the horse.

A bona-fide club whose constitution and list of members has been approved by the stewards of the Jockey Club, is allowed to own a horse and run it in its name and colours provided it vests the legal ownership, as far as the rules of racing are concerned, in a maximum of four trustees.

Club-owned horses are great fun, but rather too remote to give more than the mildest taste of the real pleasure of ownership, and it is not in the least surprising that partnerships, and particularly syndicates, have increased dramatically in recent years. If two, three or four people share the ownership of a horse, a partnership must be registered detailing the proportions each owns in the horse. Although each partner is held jointly responsible for fees and other payments, entries must be made in the name of the one with the largest share. Where they hold equal shares or there is no clear majority shareholder, they must enter the horse under the same 'owner's' name throughout the season.

The rules of syndicates are even more complex. The syndicate must consist of not more than twelve people, all of whom must be approved by the Jockey Club, as must the legal agreement between them drawn up by a solicitor and signed by all concerned. As part of that agreement, the twelve members must agree to lease the horse to a 'partnership' of three or four of their number, who will assume all the responsibilities of ownership under the rules, in the same way as do the trustees of a club-owned horse. The Jockey Club stewards must be satisfied that the control and management of the horse is in the hands of the syndicate members in whom the legal ownership of the horse is vested, or in the hands of the trainer.

Syndicates, and the other forms of multiple ownership, are a good thing for racing. This is self-evident. With bloodstock prices, and training and feeding costs rising all the time, fewer and fewer people are able to afford to buy their own racehorse, yet the number of people who wish they could do so has probably never been greater. It will get higher still as the age of automation continues to shorten the working week and increase the amount of leisure time available to the average man. Once he has paid for his one-twelfth share, which with the present upward trend in bloodstock prices could well prove a good investment in itself, our average syndicate member can enjoy, for the weekly outlay many already spend on smoking, all the thrills and fascination of ownership. He can derive as much fun from a share in a humble five-year-old gelding in the lower regions of the central handicap as the aristocrat derives from his classics contender. Syndicates are bringing into racing hundreds of men and women who would not otherwise have begun to contemplate ownership, which can only be for the long-term benefit of the sport. It enables them to put their toe in the water, as it were, without the risk of being financially submerged.

An astonishing number of syndicate members hold shares in more than one horse. Some of them could probably afford to buy a single horse outright and put it into training, but prefer to have an interest in half-a-dozen or more instead. This is in many ways a wise policy, for they not only spread their risks, but by casting their net wide, increase their chances of hitting the jackpot. It is better by far to have a share in several decent horses than be the outright owner of one that perpetually runs unplaced. Horses of all kinds are now being syndicated, but the majority fall into the £1,500–£2,500 price bracket, working out at between £150 and £250 per share, and some have met with considerable success, although the day of the first syndicate-owned Derby winner still seems a long way off.

The methods used by the different syndicate organisers to cover training and racing costs are many and varied. Some charge a fixed monthly fee, plus an extra £2 or £3 whenever the horse runs; others, like the Goodwood Bloodstock Agency and the Racegoer's Club syndicates, work on the basis of an annual lump sum payment which covers both the initial cost of a share and a year's expenses. But whatever the system it is now obligatory to submit details of all accounts—including the initial purchase of the horse—to the Jockey Club before approval can be granted.

Most people would agree that a spread of syndication, properly organised and controlled, is what racing needs and the public wants. As John Banks, the former bookmaker who is now running half-a-dozen syndicated horses through his Sporting Club International, says: 'The David Robinsons and the Lady Beaverbrooks will not be around forever. Syndicates stimulate interest in racing, and they also give the smaller owner a chance.'

There is no doubt that for the racing authorities, syndicates also present problems, not all of them immediately obvious to the layman. Hence the tiresome legal formalities and the seemingly complex rules and regulations involved in the registration of a syndicate. The dangers of unscrupulous types moving in to make excessive profits out of unsuspecting shareholders were the cause for a general tightening up of the rules in 1973. Eventually, syndicate managers will no doubt be licensed by the Jockey Club in the same way as trainers and jockeys, with a set code of conduct to govern their work. Such legislation would be welcomed by all straightforward organisations, who after all would have nothing to lose.

Alongside the ever-increasing popularity of multiple ownership, another trend is becoming more evident in European racing: the 'professional' owner. This modern breed, already well known in the United States, is exemplified best in Britain by the publicity-shy figure of Mr David Robinson, who became a millionaire with the TV rentals boom of the mid-fifties, and then turned to racing to apply the same highly successful business methods to the business of owning a string of racehorses. There have always been owners on a large scale, but most of them have been very rich men to whom money was no object, and while they appeared to win vast sums their long-term operations were usually far from profitable in the strictly commercial sense.

The hit-or-miss methods of the majority of owners were just not good enough for Robinson, who is the sort of man who sees no point in doing anything, even as a hobby, unless you do it properly. His racing organisation is an example to anyone contemplating ownership on even the most modest scale.

All the Robinson horses were purchased, for unlike almost

every large-scale owner before him he has no interest in the breeding side of the industry, except as it applies to horses he is thinking of buying! A team of experts advises him on every aspect of ownership, from breeding to race planning. Known as Robinson's Rangers, they meet each Sunday in the Operations Room of his private training establishment at Newmarket. Breeding and form experts go through the sales catalogues and mark off possible purchases. Others, including a former top trainer and a qualified vet, view the animals and make their recommendations. Any horse with an 'if' about it is automatically rejected. A private agent bids for those which survive all stages of his scrutiny, and fifty additions are made to the string each year.

Every Robinson horse in training is given a colour grading according to ability: red for outstanding, blue for good and green for fair. All the two-year-olds are graded red to begin with and regraded after they have shown their ability on the racecourse. After that only their running in races will get them promotion or demotion. The real point of the grading system is that courses are also graded, and as a general rule red class horses will run only on the red courses (the Robinson team rate ten in this category), blue horses at the twelve blue tracks and the rest at the others. The only exceptions are made when a middle- or low-grade meeting stages a more valuable race than usual. Then a higher grade horse might be aimed for it. Jockeys are graded in the same way.

Before the Sunday conference the trainer goes through the programmes for future events and makes his suggestions about possible entries and running plans. These are then thoroughly discussed, with the final decision being taken by Robinson himself. At the conference, the Operations Room looks like a scene from one of those films about the Battle of Britain. One wall is covered with a list of all the Robinson horses aged three or more. The two-year-olds have another wall to themselves. And each horse, as well as being positioned in its correct grading category, has its form figures, right up to date, attached to its name so its progress can be ascertained at a glance. Plaques alongside the horses' names denote suggested entries, pegs denote definite runners.

Such depth of expertise, commonplace in decision making in most businesses with a much smaller turnover than the Robinson empire, is almost completely foreign to racing, where professionalism, in Britain at any rate, has almost always been a dirty word. Jockeys were first to adopt the professional approach, and were despised for it. Since the war, most trainers have been forced to do so or go broke, and the result has been a stream of bright young men who have revolutionised the training scene. Even racing's ruling body has had to admit some kind of professionalism, and with the Levy Board becoming ever more powerful the days of the Jockey Club in its present voluntary-service state as the sport's supreme authority must be numbered. But the breeding industry, and far more so the owners, are the last bastions of amateurism in British racing. The former will cling to this doubtful status at the peril of their country's place in the bloodstock markets of the world. Owners with money to burn have every right to set light to it however they wish, provided the smoke does not upset their neighbours. But they will find the going harder and harder as professionalism creeps in.

Inevitably, Robinson's highly organised and very successful methods were sneered at by racing's traditionalist majority when he first arrived on the scene. Now many of those who muttered about 'supermarket methods ruining the sport' have to admit the effectiveness of those methods. To the punters, Robinson is a real hero. They know his horses are always doing their best to win. They know that his horses rarely have anything but a good chance of success since, except perhaps for their first few outings as two-year-olds when still unknown quantities, they are always running in their own class or slightly below it. And they know that the decision to run in a particular race has not been made because Aunt Mabel fancies the idea of having a runner at Goodwood, but is the result of a cogently argued case put forward by a team of men who are experts in their various fields. In the uncertain world of racing, what more could any punter wish for? And in the risky business of racehorse ownership, what better model could anyone seek?

6

The Trainer's Art

Stated in its most basic form, the art of training a racehorse is simple: to enable, with the best possible care, feeding and exercise, a horse to race to the very best of its ability. But like so many other easy-sounding jobs in life, there is far more to training than most people would imagine. It is all too easy to see only the glamour, the champagne celebrations, the newspaper headlines, and the celebrity owners handing out lavish presents after a win in some important race. What many people miss, or choose to ignore, are the long hours with little time for relaxation; the tedious, seemingly endless miles of travelling; above all the worry. It is all very well to look at champions such as Brigadier Gerard, Mill Reef or Nijinsky and say 'With material like that, how could any trainer fail?' The answer is: very easily! Of course it is easier to succeed with good horses, and the three mentioned are among the best this century, but it is probably true to say that even champions like these could have been ruined if they had not been handled in the right way. And what is the right way? There you have the problem, for there are almost as many 'right ways' to train as there are racehorses.

Imagine, too, the mental strain of being responsible round the clock for animals worth thousands of pounds, and with a potential stud value far exceeding their present value. Victory or defeat in the Derby alone can make a difference of a million pounds to a horse's value. So if the trainer permits himself a little smile as his charge is led into the winner's enclosure at Epsom by his blissful owner, do not envy him his moment of glory. Rest assured he has paid for it, not only in expert knowledge and skill, but with hours of mental and physical toil.

A trainer is traditionally racing's jack of all trades: an expert horseman, of course, but also a bit of a vet, something of a psychologist, a memory man, and a competent organiser. The description we gave of the average National Hunt trainer in *Over the Sticks* fits his flat counterpart equally well:

> As well as being responsible for his horses fifty-two weeks in the year, he must see that dozens of instructions from the Jockey Club and its stewards are carried out; he must be physically capable of working from dawn until late at night as a matter of normal routine, and of standing the strain of travelling anything up to thirty or forty thousand miles a year; to know his way around a form book; and to have the diplomacy to deal with anxious, over-zealous or downright impatient owners, as well as possessing the authority to run his stable and its staff with discipline and efficiency.

In all but the smallest establishments nowadays, it is usual for most of the detailed office work to be taken off the trainer's shoulders, either by a helpful wife or daughter, or a paid secretary. Racing, like almost everything else in the modern world, involves an ever-increasing amount of paperwork, and given the present system of entries, declarations, forfeits and general form-filling, it would be almost impossible for one man to cope with it all even if he gave up sleeping altogether!

At the same time, three main factors are combining to alter the traditional role of a trainer: the modern trend towards specialisation, the importance of efficient handling of accounts, and the growth of syndicate-ownership. Finance is at the root of all three.

Before 1939 most trainers had as their patrons wealthy men with no inclination to quibble over the bills provided their horses won a race or two at the right sort of meetings. Labour was cheap, and in many cases shamelessly exploited; there was far less paperwork. Admittedly, prize money was much lower, but so, too, were costs. In fact, bearing in mind how far the value of the pound has dropped since 1938, the average weekly training bill of five guineas at that time seems remarkably high compared with today's average of twenty to twenty-five pounds.

Writing in the weekly newspaper *The Racehorse* shortly after his retirement in October 1971, Joe Hartigan, who gave up training after eighteen years because he could 'no longer afford to lose a large sum of money each year in order to carry on the job which I enjoy and which I am well qualified to do', pointed out that before the war the average training fee per horse was approximately double the average wage of his paid staff. At 1974 rates that would mean a basic fee of at least £50 per horse each week, and few trainers today would remain in business very long if they attempted to charge such a sum!

Staff costs are not the only major item of expenditure, either. Even trainers charging their owners £35 or more a week as a basic training fee will be working on profit margins that would be laughed out of court by most business executives. The cost of some items are simply passed on to owners as extras—shoeing, for example. A racehorse needs a new set of shoes at least once a month and special racing plates—lighter aluminium-type shoes —for each race it runs. The owner would pay for these, and usually to insure his horse, too, but the trainer is still left with a hair-raising list of expenses that must come out of whatever profit he can make. He will need saddles (at least £40 new) bridles, lungeing reins and numerous other assorted items of tack, for instance. A basic set for the smallest yard would set him back well over a thousand pounds.

Then there is his fuel and heating bill, which will be far bigger than most people's, and to take just one further example of runaway expenditure, his telephone bill. With so much of his business inevitably conducted on the telephone, this will be astronomical. Another 'hidden' expense that is not generally appreciated, even by some owners who have had horses for years, is the bill for repairs. Horses are constantly kicking out stable doors, or damaging walls and posts. One we came across recently had a craving for the woollen rugs which are used to keep them warm in bad weather, or when in the parade ring. He happily chewed his way through £40 or £50 worth before his trainer, in desperation, tucked him up for the night in old sacks instead!

In the bigger centres there are gallops fees to be paid, and these can be high. At Epsom, for example, they are £25 per year per horse, at Newmarket closer to £40. The rapid rise in food costs generally in the early seventies has inevitably been reflected in the price of animal foodstuffs—the biggest single item on the debit side of a trainer's budget after salaries. Between 1972 and 1973 Australian oats went up from around £44 a ton to more than £50; English oats from below £30 to around £45 a ton. And a big stable would probably get through between three and four tons of oats every week.

VAT was another burden imposed in 1973 which trainers have had to pass on to owners. Although the rate of 8 per cent does not apply by any means to every item on the trainer's bill, it would not be far out to suggest that the introduction of the new tax system has added at least 5 per cent to the amount most trainers have to charge their patrons.

The Levy Board subsidises the cost of transporting horses to meetings by a system of travel allowances, paid where the single-journey distance involved is more than fifty miles. The current rates are as follows (distances being calculated on a one-way basis 'as the crow flies' plus 25 per cent):

Between 51 and 150 miles: £3.50 fixed allowance, plus 10p for each mile in excess of 51;

Between 151 and 300 miles: £18.50 plus 10p for each mile in excess of 151;

For 301 miles and over: £37.50 plus 10p for each mile in excess of 301 miles, subject to an overall maximum of £46.

The allowance is payable in respect of all horses declared at the 'overnight declaration' stage which are transported all or part of the way to the course, whether or not they actually run and even if the meeting is abandoned.

Some trainers make a point of weighing horses before the journey and then again when they get home, using a weighing platform rather like those one sometimes sees on a railway station. The comparison in weight can tell the trainer a great deal about the horse's condition and how hard a race he had, or in the case of a poor traveller, how much the journey took out of him. Horses can lose an amazing amount of weight in a race, as much as two stone in some cases. The other guide to how hard a race a horse has had is the way he 'eats up' when he gets home, but this is less reliable as a yardstick. Weight comparison, too, can often be useful before and after a serious training gallop, for it is an indication of how much effort the horse was putting in during the trial and, consequently, how valid any form line gained from it might be.

The number of racehorse owners with money to burn is rapidly diminishing. A trainer lucky enough to acquire a wealthy client nowadays is more likely than not to discover that he is also a wary, cost-conscious businessman who will rightly expect his trainer to run his business in the most efficient manner, and thereby give the best value for his training fees. A racing manager, working for an owner with a number of horses, probably in two or more establishments, or an assistant trainer for the man who prefers working with horses than with the form book, is often the answer. He will handle the entries and declarations, jockey bookings and details of partnerships and syndicate registrations where they apply, leaving the trainer to concentrate on his principal task: to ensure that the horses themselves are at their peak on the day of their chosen races. Mr David Robinson's organisation, mentioned in the previous chapter, is probably the best current example of this kind of set-up, but it can work equally well on a much smaller scale.

If efficiency in the managing of the trainer's horses is increasingly important, efficiency in the handling of his accounts and book-keeping is absolutely vital. A very substantial amount of capital is required to set up as trainer nowadays, and this can apply also to even the smallest establishment if one includes the cost of buying or converting premises for the purpose. Before the war, most leading trainers were men of ample means who could afford the sort of extended credit that nowadays would put a trainer out of business within six months. Even the best owners, however, will not pay their bills until they receive them: hence the need for a thoroughly efficient office and, in all but the smallest establishments, a full-time secretary.

F

Another area in which enlightened members of the training profession are becoming much more aware, is what might loosely be called public relations. Most leading trainers are commendably open with members of the racing press about future plans and the well-being of their star horses. Many have welcomed members of the Racegoers Club on tours of their stables and the fact that these stable visits are among the most popular of the club's activities shows what a grand job the trainers concerned are doing for the image of the sport as a whole.

Epsom trainer Brian Swift added a new dimension to racing publicity when he launched at the start of the 1974 season a unique bulletin designed to keep the racing press, and through them the general public, up-to-date with news about his Loretta Lodge stable and the plans for its horses. His bulletins include objectives for the various horses in the yard, jockey bookings, and comments on the running of his horses that are not shown in the form book, as well as news items about owners and the stable staff involved with each horse turned out to race. It was a unique idea, designed both to foster a team spirit between the owners, jockeys and stable staff and to keep the public informed. 'After all, the public sustain the whole racing industry', says Swift, 'and with more horses in training than ever before the task of the racing journalist in keeping them in touch becomes more demanding. I hope this helps in some small way.'

It was stated earlier in this chapter that there were probably as many different 'right ways' to train a racehorse as there are racehorses. Every horse is an individual and to adapt an old saying, one horse's tonic is another horse's poison. Half-a-dozen horses of identical age and ability given precisely the same food and training routine for a month would show vastly different results at the end of the period. Two would probably have thrived, two more would have made only average development and the other two 'gone backward' to an alarming extent. To make matters even more complicated, the ideal routine for a particular horse is not always evident from his outward appearance. Finding the magic formula is a mixture of intuition, patience and experiment. A successful trainer must not only have a flair for getting to know the individual likes and dislikes of each one of his horses, he must also be adaptable enough to admit his inevitable mistakes and always be ready to try a new routine when it is clear he is not getting the right results.

Although individual trainers differ considerably in their methods, the basic daily pattern of any large stable is much the same : an early-morning start, with the lads starting work at about 7.00am, followed by the exercising of the 'first string' which will usually consist of the horses being prepared for races in the near future. The other horses may be worked later, or perhaps given a little gentle road work, but for the most part the rest of the day at the stable itself will be devoted to grooming, cleaning out, getting horses ready for visits from the blacksmith or vet, and finally preparing and serving the main meal of the day for the horses—the evening one—and bedding them down for the night.

Most trainers will, in fact, see very little of all this. They will probably watch the important work in the morning, then there are decisions to make about horses that might be running next day, or in four days time, the two important stages in the British system of declaring runners. After this the trainer will usually have to be off to the races, leaving the stable routine to his head lad and the office work to his secretary, until he returns in the evening to inspect the horses and cope with any problems that may have arisen during his absence.

At the racecourse, the travelling head lad, and the other lads who have gone with him, will look after the horses. The trainer's main task is usually to look after the owners, to make sure they are enjoying themselves, discuss prospects, and conduct the inevitable post-mortem according to how their particular horses perform. The trainer is required by the rules of racing to make a formal declaration of his runners not less than forty-five minutes before their race, naming the jockey who will ride each horse and the weight at which he will ride. Most trainers will also supervise the final preparation and saddling of each horse for its race and then accompany the owner into the parade ring.

If necessary he will brief the jockey on the sort of race he wants him to ride.

Inevitably, as the sport has become more and more of a business, organisation more sophisticated and labour more expensive and hard to come by, a trainer with a stable of any size nowadays must act more like a general dealing with an army, or a managing director with his business than the man of toil he often was in the past. His main function is to take overall responsibility, but to delegate most of the routine work to trusted subordinates. He will decide the tactics to bring the best results from each of his charges, but he must rely on others to put them into effect.

A detailed programme of work will be mapped out for each horse, and the amount of exercise it has on any given day will depend on the physical needs of the horse and the proximity of his next race. Horses are rarely if ever galloped flat out on their home training grounds. Most trainers prefer them to be kept on the bit while working, but obviously if anything is to be discovered about the horse at all he must be pushed out a little every now and again. The ideal most trainers strive for, especially when training a horse for a big race, is to bring him to a point just a fraction short of his peak so that there is still something extra to be called upon on the big day itself.

This gauging of a horse's fitness is one of the most difficult aspects of a trainer's job. Some hardy animals seem to thrive on a really busy life. They can be brought to a peak on the gallops, and will keep their condition for two or three races. Others, however, tend to go 'off the boil' quickly and the timing of their preparation is crucial. Often a horse of this nature is said to have 'left the race on the gallops', meaning that he hit his peak at home and was 'over the top' when it came to the race itself. If this happens more than once or twice with the same horse it is a serious reflection on the trainer.

Just as every horse will eat differently, so, too, will they react differently to training. Some require weeks of work before being anywhere near their best; with others the lightest of preparation is enough to put them in fine fettle. No trainer, incidentally, will work the same two horses together regularly. If he did, the better of the two would finish up by giving his stable companion an inferiority complex.

Sunday—still a blank day for racing in Britain—is the day on which many trainers work out running plans for the coming week, often in conjunction with the stable's main jockey. Entries for future events need to be made, too. In most cases these have to be done three weeks before the race, although for many big races entries are required much earlier, and in the case of the Derby, more than a year before!

Almost certainly a programme will have been mapped out well in advance for the best horses in the stable, but the best-laid schemes can go wrong, and it is always advisable to make several alternative entries in case a late switch is desired for any reason. With the moderate or poor horses in the yard it is usual to make a wide range of entries and then a decision where and when to run can be made when the opposition and other factors are known.

However long they have been established, trainers must apply each year for a renewal of their licence to train from the Jockey Club. Before a licence is granted to a new applicant his character and his stables will be put under close scrutiny, and he must submit a list of the horses he has in his care. The Jockey Club covers both codes of racing, and whereas separate licences were previously needed, dual licences, covering both codes, were introduced in February 1975.

Feeding is another vital part of the trainer's art. It is not enough to simply buy enough top-quality food, divide it up between the animals in the yard and leave them to get on with it. In eating, as in their work requirements, horses differ considerably. Some will eat anything in sight, others will need coaxing, and cajoling into eating what is best for them. It is not simply a question of size, either. Some horses, like some human beings, can eat any amount of food but retain a natural leanness. Others put on weight with almost every mouthful.

This question of size can often mislead the inexpert onlooker, or even buyer, at yearling sales. Big, healthy-looking individuals are not necessarily the excellent racing prospects they seem, for much of their size can be 'grass fatness' which must be lost before they start any serious training. The danger is that if this process is hurried, the muscle which the training builds up will go on in all the wrong places. Or, more seriously, too much work too soon, will cause breathing difficulties which could lead to serious infirmity. The small, lean yearling may not appear so promising in the sales ring, but he gives his trainer the oppor- tunity to carefully build up his muscle with the minimum of risk.

Inner cleanliness, says the advertisement, comes first. And while liver salts are not on the prescribed diet of any horse we know, it is true that an animal obviously glowing with health from his external appearance is equally fit internally. A horse's droppings are the best guide to his general condition, so these must be observed at regular intervals by the trainer, or more likely, his head lad.

In training, a horse's basic diet is hay, oats and 'nuts', or 'pellets' as the concentrated food cubes now being marketed by the leading animal food firms are called. These can be used instead of the usual weekly mash of boiled barley and oats, linseed and bran, or in conjunction with it. The big advantage of 'nuts' is their ease of preparation compared with the tedious mixing of the old oats and bran, and the fact that they can be measured in exact quantities. But they are not entirely without their snags. One major animal foodstuffs firm became involved in a lengthy investigation by the Jockey Club stewards after side-effects resulting from a diet of their product had resulted in dope tests on four horses proving positive. The trainers concerned were naturally surprised, to say the least, since other horses on the same diet had been tested without producing the same results, and since four in every five of their colleagues were estimated to use similar 'nuts' without any of their horses producing a positive test.

The amount of food a horse eats will vary, of course, with the individual, but as a general guide an average flat-racing horse in training will munch its way through between twelve and sixteen pounds of concentrates and nearly the same amount of hay each day, although the amount of hay will be reduced on the day before racing. As for water, the amount it drinks will depend on how hard it has been working, but it is usually between six and ten gallons a day.

Eating, drinking and working (not necessarily in that order) are important parts of a horse's day, but they take up a very small proportion of the twenty-four hours. How he spends the remainder may not seem very important at first. Indeed, the traditional view was, or is, that it is of no consequence whatever, but this attitude is changing fast.

Most trainers realise nowadays that horses are naturally gregarious animals and full of curiosity. They love to see what is going on and they love having their day brightened by some unusual or intriguing sight such as a different sort of animal playing in or crossing through the yard, or a change in the pattern of their daily routine. Once, horses used to be shut away in their boxes for the best part of every afternoon and invariably exercised on the same bit of gallops day in day out. In a few stables this lamentable state of affairs still persists, but the majority of trainers now realise that a successful horse is usually a happy horse. They introduce informality and variety into training routines and do everything possible to lessen the boredom of the twenty or more hours a day in which a racehorse is doing virtually nothing. (See plate, p 18.)

The rows of horse boxes are usually built around a courtyard, and with the top half of his box open a horse can look out and see the comings and goings of people and other horses through-out the day. Even the most mundane activities can be of compelling interest, while many horses develop playful habits with the lads that look after them. Sometimes, for example, one will grab the rake his lad uses to clear away the dirty straw and swing it from side to side in his mouth. One horse of our acquaintance would not rest if he could see a bucket of water within reach until he had overturned it somehow.

The idea of isolating racehorses in separate compartments probably developed from the way in which stable blocks in

Britain were invariably built until recent times. Now, it is significant that many new blocks are being built in the 'American-barn' style long favoured by horsemen in the United States and in Europe. Top British trainer Peter Walwyn has most of the horses in his Lambourn yard in 'barn-style' blocks, where horses are housed in low-sided stalls under one communal roof so they can all see one another. Sussex trainer Guy Harwood has fifty horses housed like this in one huge barn, probably the first of its kind in a British racing stable. Now others are following his example. When Derek Weeden decided to move to new premises in Suffolk in 1973 he had the stable block designed on 'American-barn' style. 'With labour as it is nowadays, it saves a lot of time', he said. 'And, most important, it is warm for the horses.'

The exploits of steeplechaser Red Rum have done a great deal to kill off another long-held prejudice among British trainers: that against training horses on the seashore. The way in which the ozone in sea air can invigorate horses has never been in dispute: several big Newmarket stables regularly send their horses down to Yarmouth for a training spin on the race-course there. But even many of these trainers would not gallop their horses on the sands because it has been thought for many years that this would make them slow. The prejudice was strengthened by the evidence of a professional surveyor called in by one prominent trainer more than sixty years ago to measure the strides of selected horses galloping at full stretch, first on sands at Redcar and subsequently on their home gallops at Middleham in Yorkshire. He found that the strides of the horses on the sands covered slightly less ground than they did on the turf of Middleham Moor, and the inference drawn from his findings, rightly or wrongly, was that regular galloping on sand would shorten a horse's stride permanently.

Harry Whiteman, and Capt Charles Elsey, the doyen of the old-time Yorkshire trainers, were just two of the men who disputed this theory, and the success of trainers using the sands at places such as Dunbar, in Scotland, and Mablethorpe, in Lincolnshire, reinforce their argument. There is, too, the point that salt water is very good for toughening a horse's legs, and swimming very definitely an excellent method of putting on muscle.

Some people would take this questioning of accepted methods even further. Why have almost all excercise gallops in the morning, for instance, when racing is usually in the afternoon? The practical answer, of course, is for precisely that reason. The trainer, and probably the jockeys and apprentices who ride for him, too, will be at the races in the afternoon and not available for training sessions. Newmarket's place as the principal training centre is regarded as more an accident of history than a desirable state of affairs by others. It is true that the vast expanse of windswept heath does not bring the best out of all horses, as can be seen by the improvement shown by many of them when moved to cosier provincial or even foreign surroundings.

Other animals can be useful for trainers wanting to keep their horses lively and interested in what is going on. Some living in country areas have been known to send a flock of sheep through the yard to give the horses something new to look at. Many more have brought in goats or donkeys to keep particular horses company, and occasionally some touching friendships have resulted. One of these, between a bay gelding called Avondhu, and a donkey who was his closest companion, ended sadly. Horse and donkey were inseparable. Everywhere the horse went, meetings included, the donkey went, too. But then Avondhu was moved from Scotland to new stables in Sussex, and somehow the donkey was left behind. It was a day or two before the mistake was discovered, and in that time the donkey had made its way to the horse's stable to die of a broken heart.

7

The Forgotten Army

Lad or Girl wanted, six-and-a-half-day week, with opportunity for (unpaid) overtime. Wages well below national average. Live-in accommodation provided, but cramped and dingy; prospects of promotion very limited. Only enthusiastic, hard workers need apply.

Would you let your son or daughter take on a job like this? Of course you would not. But although you will never see 'Situations Vacant' advertisements for stable staff worded in quite this way, the dismal picture painted above is all too accurate in the vast majority of cases. There are exceptions, of course. Working conditions and living accommodation in some of Britain's top yards are very good, although even here the work is hard and poorly paid by industrial standards. There are also many smaller stables where kindness and generosity of spirit make up for shortcomings in other respects. But all too often this vast and vital 'forgotten army' is shamefully exploited, consciously or otherwise, by trainers who simply dare not risk driving owners away by increasing their fees and by officials who seem to regard stable staff as second-class citizens.

An example of the latter marred the opening in September 1973 of Sandown Park's magnificent £2 million grandstand complex. A preview day was held some days before the actual opening, to which guests from all sections of the racing world, including several leading journalists, were invited. The guests enjoyed a lavish three-course meal in the members' dining-room, while a group of stable lads who had come along with horses used to give 'life' to the publicity pictures of the new paddock had to make do with cheese sandwiches. Not only was this a very poor piece of public relations, which resulted in a great deal of bad publicity, but the incident illustrates a lack of consideration that is all too commonplace in the treatment given to these key workers in the industry. No doubt the Sandown authorities had not intended any snub to the lads; they simply did not think of them. Moreover, it should be added that the amenities and accommodation for stable lads visiting Sandown in the course of their work now is very good, unlike those at many of Britain's racecourses.

Overcrowding and lack of catering, washing and toilet facilities are the most frequent subjects of complaint and though many of the offending courses have plans for improvement, the priority given to expenditure on their welfare is, in the opinion of most stable lads at least, often far too low on the list. And here again we come up against a problem that does not exist in France or the United States, not only because racing there is more affluent but primarily because it is more centralised. Racecourses staging the number of racing days a year that most American courses average can afford to build luxury hostels for stable workers. British courses, with an average of twenty racing days a year, find it extremely difficult to finance even barely adequate accommodation. One idea under consideration is to build motel-type units at racecourses, especially those in holiday areas, which could be used by members of the public like any ordinary motel in non-racing periods. It sounds a promising suggestion.

Most stable lads in Britain, and nowadays many of the girls, too, come into racing hoping eventually to become jockeys. Before very long it becomes clear that most of them will be too heavy and they either move to jumping stables in the hope of becoming National Hunt jockeys, or carry on as stable lads with the aim of graduating one day perhaps to the position of head lad, or even assistant trainer. Each lad will have two or three horses that are his responsibility, and often they become very proud of 'their' horses: especially if they are fortunate enough to have one of the stable stars among their charges. As the months go by they get to know every detail about the likes and dislikes of their horses for they not only feed them, water them and muck them out every day, they usually accompany them when they travel away to race and often ride them on the gallops as well. Many a jockey, wanting to know some particular aspect of a horse's character or well-being, obtains his information not from the trainer, but from the stable lad or his head lad, who often know the animal in much more detail.

If he is not required to go to a race meeting, a lad will usually start his day at around 7.00am, feed and muck out his horses and tack up the first one for the gallops and then go out with the string before he has his own breakfast. After that there may be a second visit to the gallops, or some road work, followed by general tidying up around the yard until lunchtime. Most big stables give their lads the afternoon off, calling them in again at 4 or 5pm to help with the evening meal, more clearing up and then bedding the horses down for the night.

In general, the horses will go out during the season every day except Sunday, but will only be seriously worked on two or three days out of the six. Modern practice is all against the rigid routine, but a typical week's activity would be something like this: Monday, road work; Tuesday, cantering on the gallops; Wednesday, gallop; Thursday, road work; Friday, cantering and Saturday, another good gallop. Obviously this programme would be varied to fit in with a horse's racing. If he was to run on the Thursday, for instance, he would work normally until about the Monday before the race. Then on Tuesday he would have some quiet exercise, followed by a sharp workout on the Wednesday. If the meeting entailed an overnight journey this final workout might be left until the morning of the race and carried out on the course. Then, back home after the race, he would have a rest day and probably another quiet day or two, depending on temperament, before picking up the normal routine once more.

In the United States, there is not the same link between stable work and a jockey's career as in Britain. Consequently, stable lads there tend to be much bigger, tougher types, far more capable of carrying out the many heavy chores involved in stable work than

British lads are. But the system is not without its drawbacks, principal among them being that because they have not spent years 'doing their two' (or three) like their British counterparts, American jockeys tend to be simply riders, and not horsemen. It may be no coincidence that world-class American-born jockeys are few and far between.

The head lad is a key figure in any training establishment, and in a few cases the actual trainer in all but the name on a licence. He is the behind-the-scenes 'sergeant major' who organises the work of the stable, the man who actually sees things are done. The head lad will usually be on duty almost an hour before the rest, giving the horses their small early-morning feed. While most of the team is out on the gallops, he will usually stay in the yard, carrying out minor veterinary work or organising odd jobs that need to be done. A good head lad has inevitably worked his way up from the bottom and will be able to turn his hand to almost anything from tending a horse's bruised leg to replating one in an emergency if the farrier has not turned up. When they are not sent away, it is usually the head lad who breaks in the yearlings, too.

In the bigger stables there will also be a travelling head lad, who assumes his duties at the races, often doubling as driver of the trainer's horsebox. On busy days he will act as the trainer's representative, being responsible for declaring the horses and their weights, preparing them for their races and looking after them afterwards before driving home again to start a round of vital chores such as filling hay nets and checking that the next day's runners have had their plates fitted and the appropriate colours are ready.

Most trainers prefer their horses to travel to a meeting on the day of their race if possible, and this will often mean a very early start to the day for them and the lads concerned. A Sussex-trained horse with a date at Catterick or Haydock, for example, would be having his early-morning feed at around 4.30am, for except where a long stop is planned it would be inadvisable to eat on the journey. The 'restaurant car' horsebox is just not on. There are other difficulties, besides the eating arrangements. A colt ought not to be boxed up beside a filly, for example. They would probably upset one another on the way.

Like human beings, horses vary considerably in their reaction to travelling. Some would seemingly be quite happy to live in a horsebox. Others invariably travel badly, and rarely produce their best form after a long journey. These, and possibly his two-year-olds, too, are the horses a trainer would send on well in advance of the meeting, so that they can stay overnight, maybe two or three nights in the stables at the racecourse, or at some friendly trainer's yard near the course, and settle down in their new surroundings before the big race.

The job of travelling head lad, like most others in racing, entails a six-day week for most of the year, heavy work and a position of considerable responsibility. Yet the average travelling head lad receives, apart from free housing, little more than the average farm worker except for his share of the stable's 2·5 per cent cut of prize money won: in all but the most successful yards a total of less than £35 a week gross. And the head lad is likely to get only a pound or two more.

The lot of the ordinary stable lad is equally unattractive in the purely commercial sense. He has not the responsibility of the head lad or travelling head lad, but still works what amounts to a seven-day week for most of the year for a weekly wage of between £15 and £25 at current rates. Almost every lad could earn twice as much in a factory at far less risk to life and limb and in return for many fewer hours' toil.

Few do, of course, for despite all the danger and drudgery, the early hours and the long working day, there is something about the racing life, like the actor's life, that makes the purely financial returns comparatively unimportant. Say to an outsider that the racing world is similar in many ways to the theatre and he will immediately start talking about the glamour of Ascot and the drama of a big-race photo-finish. To most people in racing, the truer parallel would be between the struggling repertory actor waiting patiently for the break that will turn him into a star overnight, and the humble stable lad dreaming of the chance ride that will rocket him into the headlines as the new Lester Piggott.

Smile if you will, but the day such dreams fade for good, and lads collectively demand strict cash compensation for the very valuable work they do, will be an expensive day indeed for racing.

8

The Headquarters

The principal training centres in Britain for flat racing are Newmarket, Epsom, and the Lambourn area of Berkshire in the south, and the district around the Yorkshire town of Malton, in the north. Newmarket, home of the Jockey Club, is the official headquarters of British racing. As well as two racecourses, it houses the National Stud, the Equine Research Centre, Tattersalls' Park Paddocks, where the major bloodstock sales take place, and numerous private studs, as well as more than forty training establishments catering between them for something like 1,600 horses. Charles II is generally accorded the credit for giving this somewhat obscure little Suffolk town its very special position in the world of racing, although it is more than possible that even without the royal accolade Newmarket's topography alone would have done the same. Acre upon acre of heathland provide gallops in plenty virtually the whole year round, and one of these areas, a vast tract of land lying between the main roads to Norwich and Bury St Edmunds, known as the Limekilns, is reputed to be the finest in the world.

The Limekilns, and all the other gallops areas on the Heath, were owned until a few years ago by the Jockey Club, who transferred them in 1968, together with their other lands, to the Newmarket Estates and Property Company whose first board of directors happened to be the then members of the Jockey Club. Trainers pay an annual fee, known as a heath tax, of £37.50 for each horse of two years old and more, and £4.50 for each yearling in their stables, and strict rules are laid down about training on the Heath. No horses are allowed there before 5am or after 4pm (midday on Sundays), and not all gallops are available every day. A list of those which may be used is posted the previous afternoon on the official notice board outside the Jockey Club Rooms in the High Street. (See plate, p 17.)

It is impossible to remain long in this lovely town with its bustling main street brimming with racing personalities; its innumerable pubs and cafés seething with racing gossip, without catching some of the excitement of the racecourse: even when the nearest race meeting is hundreds of miles away. For the price of several cups of coffee you can receive a cast-iron tip for virtually everything on four legs that is running that day, and more than a few that are not, but it is all part of the romance of racing. There is a legend in Newmarket that even the sausages sold in the butchers' shops are made from Derby winners. And the locals can retail the story without a flicker of a smile. It could not happen anywhere else, and it all adds to the unique character of the place.

Not even the most disinterested spectator could fail to be stirred by the sight of the early morning training sessions on the Heath. It is one of the most magnificent free spectacles on earth, and one that is incredibly neglected by the tourist industry. To get the full flavour you need to be up fairly early—around seven o'clock at the latest—but you will not begrudge the loss of an hour or two's lie-in. To be on the Limekilns or the racecourse side of the Heath as the sun breaks through the early morning haze of a hot summer day, and to see hundreds of thoroughbreds, collectively worth millions of pounds, cantering across the turf, or galloping in twos and threes under the watchful eye of their respective trainers; to hear the thunder of hooves as they race past and away into the distance is a memorable experience, and it would be a dull soul indeed that did not respond to its beauty.

For one small group of men, watching this glorious scene is a routine part of their daily working lives. The Newmarket work-watchers, or touts as they are sometimes called, make daily reports on the training sessions which are published in the *Sporting Life* and *Sporting Chronicle*. Ordinary racegoers who find it almost impossible to distinguish one horse from another unless it is wearing a numbered saddlecloth, or carrying a jockey whose colours they can check with their racecard, never cease to marvel at the ability of these touts to recognise at a glance almost every one of the 1,600 horses in training at Newmarket. But recognise them they can, even when, as sometimes happens, a trainer goes to elaborate lengths to put them 'off the scent'.

The touts learn to identify the newcomers in a trainer's string by means of a notebook system that is a cross between shorthand and sketching. They make an outline rather like a matchstick drawing of a horse, together with its main colouring, which can be ascertained from the official records. Then they mark on the 'skeleton' various symbols to represent particular features, or splashes of different colour, until a complete picture of the animal is built up. A few mornings' practice, with regular checks on the notebook, and before long the newcomer is instantly recognisable as soon as he comes within range of their binoculars.

The first races at Newmarket were run by Scotsmen attached to the court of King James I, who was the first monarch to unite England and Scotland under one crown by peaceful means. He was much keener on hunting and hawking than racing, but saw the wisdom of testing and improving the breed of British horses, and that racing was a way to achieve this end. The sport was already popular north of the border and the courtiers who had grown to love it there were not slow to organise similar events on the Heath. When James I hunted there, Newmarket was simply a collection of huts, but he liked the place so much that he had a palace built for himself. Others were quick to follow suit, and the town grew rapidly. James established public races in many parts of the country, usually giving a silver bell as the prize. The Scottish course of Lanark still has a centuries-old silver bell as part of the prize for one of its major races, and the name also survives in a modern race at Carlisle.

James's son, Charles I, took more than a passing interest in the sport, and in Newmarket, until the more important matter of a civil war put such frivolities out of his mind. But after the austerities of the Cromwellian era, Charles's son, Charles II, known as the Merrie Monarch, restored the monarchy; and it was his deep love of racing in general, and Newmarket in particular, that established the town once and for all as the home of the sport in Britain. Charles was no mere spectator: he is the only King of England to have ridden the winner of a race; he founded the famous Newmarket Town Plate which is still run today under its own special rules, and is commemorated in the Rowley Mile, the course over which the 2,000 Guineas is run. For 'Old Rowley' was Charles's nickname, derived from the name of his favourite hack.

The royal progress from London to Newmarket for the races in the days of Charles II was the wonder of the countryside. Noblemen, courtiers, thieves and prostitutes descended in force on the tiny town, transforming it into the fashionable capital of the country. The king built a house near his grandfather's palace for his mistress, Nell Gwynn, cunningly linking the two buildings with a secret subterranean passage. So many rich men came to Newmarket for the races that one of the most notable brothels in Europe, reputed to feature the most seductive girls in the world, regularly moved to the town for the season.

Later monarchs, especially Queen Anne, William IV, Edward VII, George V and his granddaughter, the present queen Elizabeth II, maintained the close links between royalty and racing, although Queen Elizabeth no longer has horses trained at Newmarket. Her Coronation Year Derby runner-up, Aureole, was trained by Noel Murless in his magnificent Warren Place yard, but even this was a horse leased to Her Majesty by the National Stud. Her own horses are mostly in the care of Ian Balding, at Kingsclere, in Berkshire.

King William IV, uncle of Queen Victoria, gave to the Jockey Club one of its most treasured possessions: a hoof of the great Eclipse, probably the finest racehorse ever seen in Britain, and the fountainhead of most of the best British bloodlines. The hoof, mounted on a gold salver, is used to ornament the Jockey Club tables in their premises in Newmarket High Street. It bears the inscription: 'This piece of plate with the hoof of Eclipse was presented by His Most Gracious Majesty King William the Fourth to the Jockey Club, May 1832.'

At the entrance to the town, if you approach from the direction of London and Cambridge, near the drinking fountain erected in 1910 as a memorial to Sir Daniel Cooper by his widow, is a cemetery which is a place of pilgrimage for racing folk from all over the world. Here many famous racing personalities are buried, among them the legendary Fred Archer, who joined a racing stable at the tender age of eleven and developed into one of the greatest jockeys in the world, riding nearly 3,000 winners in ten seasons. Archer, known as 'The Tinman' because of his love of money, was ruined by gambling and his life ended tragically when he shot himself in a fit of delirium a few weeks after the Cambridgeshire of 1886, in which he had been unexpectedly beaten on the favourite, St Mirren, by a head and lost a fortune as a consequence. It was a tragic waste of a great talent, all the more regrettable because Archer was still a comparatively young man when he died. There is no knowing the heights to which he could have risen, for he had wonderful ability to stay calm in the most demanding situations—and shared with Lester Piggott, probably the most talented of his successors as champion jockey, an uncanny ability to understand and get the best out of the horses he rode.

It is not only on race days that Newmarket is the centre of the racing world. Tattersalls' Sales, held in their Park Paddocks ring just down the road from Archer's last resting place, are also responsible for attracting huge crowds to the town. Here buyers from the developing racing nations, such as Japan, rub shoulders with rivals from the United States, Australia, Africa, and almost every country in Western Europe to bid for some of the cream of British bloodstock, which is still regarded as being among the best in the world. (See plate, p 71.)

The principal sales take place in December, although there are now several smaller sales at other times throughout the year. It is at the December sales, however, that the biggest transactions usually take place. The amount of money spent, and the top prices paid are in themselves a startlingly vivid barometer of the increase in bloodstock values over the years. The world record price for a public auction was paid here in 1967, when Vaguely Noble, then a two-year-old, was sold for 136,000 guineas. He went on to win the Prix de L'Arc de Triomphe the following year, so the expense proved worthwhile. In 1972, Ginevra, the first winner of the Oaks to pass through the sales ring in the year of her triumph, was 'knocked down' to an agent acting on behalf of a Japanese stud for 106,000 guineas, a new record for a mare or filly sold at an auction in Europe. An ironic touch was given to this transaction by the fact that Ginevra had been offered at Park Paddocks once before, as a yearling, but failed to reach a modest reserve and was eventually sold privately for just 2,000 guineas!

The 136,000 guineas price-tag on Vaguely Noble, later syndicated as a £2 million stallion, contrasts with the 10,000 guineas paid in the same sales ring in 1900 for Sceptre, a yearling filly who became one of the most famous mares in British racing history. The price was considered quite incredible at the time.

A team of eight auctioneers worked non-stop for nearly fifty-seven hours at the Tattersalls December Sales of 1972, to cope with a catalogue of 1,500 horses in five days. At the end of it all they could look back on some staggering figures. Altogether, 1,228 lots were sold to buyers from thirty different countries for 6,841,528 guineas—an average of 5,571 guineas for each horse sold. The previous year's average had been 4,286 guineas, itself a record, but nearly 30 per cent short of the new figure. And, as the *Sporting Life* pointed out: 'Even these figures cannot convey the real extent of the extraordinary inflation, for the consensus of opinion was that the 1972 catalogue was considerably inferior to its predecessor. Keep that last point in mind and the spectacular increase in demand was amazing!'

Much of the increase was due to the activities of the buyers from Japan, a country with virtually no racing at all until the 1950s but now one of the most prosperous racing nations in the world. It was reliably estimated that Japanese buyers paid more than a million and a quarter pounds for one hundred horses, including Ginevra, of course, and the increasing tempo of

Japanese bloodstock buying is well illustrated by a comparison of that one and a quarter million spent at just one sale with the total of £5 million spent by them on British bloodstock during the whole of the previous fifteen years.

The firm of Tattersalls was founded in 1766 by Yorkshireman Richard Tattersall, who organised sales of both horses and dogs on a site at Hyde Park Corner in London, and later moved to Knightsbridge, where the firm still have their London offices. Sales continued to be held in London until 1939, but after the war the whole of this side of the business was transferred to Newmarket, where the firm, which began its operations in the town by selling horses on the pavement outside the Jockey Club Rooms, had been holding regular sales at Park Paddocks since 1870. The distinctive rotunda, with its statue of a fox, which graces the sales yard at Newmarket, was brought there from London after World War II when the firm's old Knightsbridge premises were demolished to make way for the new office block in which they are housed today.

9

Makin' and Breakin'

Every yearling that arrives in a trainer's yard is regarded by his proud owner as the natural successor to Brigadier Gerard. Whether he cost 18,000 guineas or eighty, his owner will cherish the hope that he has discovered a new superstar. The trainer, knowing that in Britain only 7 per cent of horses in training so much as earn their keep in an average year, and that nowhere is the happy proportion more than 40 per cent, can be pardoned for making a more realistic appraisal of his new charge. He will want to temper the owner's natural optimism without damping it down too much. After all, with statistics such as those just mentioned, optimism of the highest order is vital for ownership, and without owners the trainer would be out of a job.

The trainer will, almost invariably, have helped to buy the horse, either privately or at one of the big bloodstock sales, so he will know something about it before he actually takes it in. He will be reasonably happy about the horse's breeding and physical make-up, but however attractive his looks, the animal will have to learn to gallop straight and fast if he is to make the grade in the harshly competitive world of flat racing.

The trainer will not be the only one casting a critical eye on the new arrival when he emerges from the horsebox at his new home. Stable lads love to study the new additions to the yard, trying to pick out the ones that will turn out best and those who will fall by the wayside. And even these experts can be wide of the mark with their predictions, for very often the best-looking horse at this stage turns out to be the slowcoach of the party.

All the yearlings that come into the yard will have been handled by people at the studs where they were bred and will have become accustomed to a headcollar. Many, however, will still be very nervous: perhaps they have not been particularly kindly treated; maybe they are simply highly strung. Others may have developed a stubborn or nasty trait because those looking after them were frightened of them and they have been used to getting their own way. Firmness and kindness are as important to the upbringing of young horses as they are to young human beings!

Education experts and psychologists are putting the emphasis increasingly nowadays on the importance of the 'pre-school' years in a child's life. Similarly, the eighteen months or so of his life which a young horse spends before he begins the serious business of actual training has a vital bearing on his future. It is in this period that his character is largely formed, and without the right sort of attitude a horse is unlikely to win races, however fast he can run. Attitude can affect more than simply his racing life, too. It is generally accepted that his remarkable temperament played as big a part in champion Mill Reef's survival to start his £2 million career at stud as the skill of the surgeon and the devotion of those who nursed him after his tragic accident on the training gallops.

Because of the increasing awareness of the importance of the formative years in a horse's life, more and more trainers are relinquishing the 'breaking in' of their young charges to expert horsemen who specialise in this vital, demanding art. These kindly, incredibly patient men are the unsung heroes of racing. Their work, painstakingly carried out in quiet farms and livery stables a world away from the glamour and tumult of the race-course, can make or mar a thoroughbred worth thousands. 'Breaking' is an ugly term, and gives a totally misleading impression of their work. 'Making' would in most cases be far more appropriate.

From the time he is born to the day he begins the 'breaking' process, a horse will have spent most of his life grazing in a field. Now, before he can be taught to gallop fast and straight he must become accustomed to having a rider on his back, and all the paraphernalia that goes with it. The first piece of strange new equipment he will meet is the bridle. The first bridle's bit is often fitted with strips of metal hanging down like a bunch of keys on a key ring. The idea is that the horse will play with these with his tongue, becoming used to the bit in the process. At the same time a large cloth strap, called a roller, will be fitted round his belly, to get him used to the idea of the girth strap of the saddle which is the next item to be introduced.

When the 'breaker' judges the horse is ready, he carefully places the saddle on the animal's back, quietly and with the minimum of fuss. The girths are done up quite loosely until he is fully accustomed to this strange thing on his back, and he is then walked around for a while, with stops every so often during which the girths are tightened, just a little at a time to avoid frightening him. Once a horse gets to know exactly what is happening when a saddle is put on he tends to blow his belly out as it is being fitted, so that when he walks forward the girths are loose. This is why you will see horses having their girths tightened in the paddock before a race, and often again at the start.

All this time our yearling will also be going through the process of lungeing. A long rein is attached to the bridle and the horse goes round the 'breaker' in a circle in either direction, first walking, then at a trot and finally at a canter. This teaches him obedience and balance.

By this time the yearling is almost ready for the most crucial stage of all: having the rider on his back. It is no good just putting a crash helmet on some poor lad's head and shoving him into the saddle. Rodeo displays may be all the rage in Wild West shows, but they do not figure in the programme for preparing highly valuable racehorses for the career fate has chosen for them. As with so many aspects of dealing with animals, patience is the keyword. First the handler will lean across the horse's back while he is standing still. Later he lies across the saddle while a colleague holds the horse's head, both of them talking all the time to the horse to give him confidence. When he has become accustomed to this, and is still quiet, the 'rider' progresses to plenty of moving about and eventually puts his leg across so that he is in a sitting position. Once more there is a great deal of talking and no sudden movements, so that the horse has time to take in what is happening and not be frightened by it all. Soon he will be led round by the lad at his head with the rider still in the saddle, and if he is at all intelligent, quickly gets used to the pressures from the man on his back and their meaning: pressure with the legs and on the reins signalling turns in that direction.

Now the horse is ready to return to his trainer to learn about racing itself. His first weeks in training will be spent quietly walking or trotting around the roads, then it is time for learning to gallop. An old or quiet horse will lead the young ones: a male, for obvious reasons if there are colts in the party, and they will follow and copy him as he progresses from a walk to a trot and then a canter. Gradually the pace is built up until they know more or less how to gallop. There will be no question at this stage of one horse racing against another, and the gallops would never be more than three furlongs or so. But as the start of the flat season approaches the trainer begins to inject a more serious tone into the proceedings.

At this stage some of the young horses will clearly need to grow more, to fill out their frames, before they can be seriously trained. These will probably be kept back for the late summer or autumn, or even for the following year. The trainer will now concentrate on the nippy characters, the 'early sorts' who have been quick to grasp the idea of racing, and are speedy enough to suggest they might win a race or two early on.

His first gallops will be in a line of horses, and then upsides another, to get him used to having to race in close company. Nearer the day of his planned first race comes the most important gallop so far: a test run against one of the stable's older horses who is a reliable 'yardstick'. Until this trial the trainer can only judge his youngster's ability in relation to the other inexperienced members of his team, and they could all be really good horses or, more probably, possess just average ability. When a two-year-old making his racecourse debut is the subject of a big gamble, it is usually on the strength of a good display in a trial such as this. However hard the trainer tries to keep the secret, word usually gets round, especially in one of the bigger training centres.

Before the newcomer can make his debut, however, he has one more important lesson to learn : he must become used to starting stalls. He will start by being quietly walked through a wooden frame, built like the stalls but with no door at the back or front. When he is thoroughly used to this he will progress to a set of actual stalls. At first the doors are left open and the horse again simply walked through so that he is not frightened by the strange contraption. After a time some banging of the doors and frame is introduced to simulate the atmosphere of the racecourse. Later the doors are closed, and then quietly opened as the horses still walk out; then ultimately the full procedure of the doors flying open and the horse leaping out into a gallop is attained. Too much excitement at this stage can frighten a horse off stalls altogether, but once again patience and quiet perseverence can pay big dividends, especially in the early part of the season when a good start in a two-year-old sprint can make the difference between victory and defeat.

10

The Race Riders

Jockeys are the glamour boys of racing. While the majority of the sport's professionals work quietly behind the scenes, either at the course or in the training stables, the jockeys are constantly in the spotlight, their work open to the most minute scrutiny, not only from binocular-aided spectators in the stands but the far-seeing eye of the television or patrol film camera as well. The average racegoer goes to the races to have a bet on the horses 'live' instead of in his local betting shop. His wife usually goes primarily to see the horses and the jockeys—and not necessarily in that order. It is easy to understand why, of all racing's professionals, it is the jockey with whom the ordinary man identifies himself. The modern jockey is a highly paid character with a smart, swinging, jet-set image, operating in a high-speed world teeming with drama and excitement and peopled by wealthy men, beautiful women and valuable animals. A world where a single split-second decision can decide the destiny of more money than most working men could earn in a quarter of a century of toil. A world where a couple of minutes' work can net the equivalent of a year's salary in many a more mundane occupation.

It is not all like that, of course. There are horses to be ridden on a wet October Monday at Catterick as well as in the sunshine of Royal Ascot or the golden cauldron that is Epsom on Derby Day. At the top of the tree a jockey's life is a great one, offering substantial rewards and a fair measure of job satisfaction. But, like other professions with glamour and money at the top, the

116

competition is tremendous and only a tiny percentage of those who set out with high hopes of making the grade actually do so.

The first step for a youngster aiming to become a jockey in Britain is to get himself articled to a licensed trainer. The lad must be at least fifteen and under the age of twenty-three, and the apprentice contract he, or rather his legal guardian, signs —usually after a three-months' trial period—will bind him to that particular trainer for a minimum of three years, during which time he will be employed as a stable lad, learn the routine, ride out at exercise after a while, and eventually, if he proves good enough, graduate to riding in actual races. Life is much better for apprentices nowadays than it was in the past. As recently as the forties and fifties, the conditions in which some lads were housed, and the hours they worked, were positively Dickensian. At some British racecourses they still are, but things are gradually being improved—and not before time.

The really lucky lads find themselves articled to a trainer who has both the understanding and the patience to coach his young protégés in the art of race riding. The man with one of the finest records in this respect is Gloucestershire trainer 'Frenchie' Nicholson, whose tiny stable, nicknamed the 'rider's academy', has produced a stream of top names, including Tony Murray, Pat Eddery, Paul Cook and a likely candidate for future stardom, Chris Leonard. Nicholson, himself taught by Stanley Wootton, a master-trainer who also had the happy knack of imparting his jockeyship knowhow to his young pupils, maintains an iron discipline but softens its edges with a boyish sense of humour. His reputation, and the record of his academy's graduates, now bring him in hundreds of applications each year from youngsters dreaming of being another Tony Murray or Willie Carson. He is able to take on only a very few. 'I look for alertness, good manners and a tidy appearance first in a new applicant', he says. 'If they become too heavy then I try to help them to find another job.'

The trainer will weigh his apprentices at the start of the season in their riding gear, and make regular weight checks throughout the year. It is important to know what each lad's

riding weight is, not only for his public rides, but because
the trainer organising a private gallop wants to know exactly
what weight each horse taking part is carrying.

To begin with the lad will look after, and ride out, one of the
stable's quieter horses. Even if he is a fairly experienced rider he
will have to be trained to ride a thoroughbred. He will have to
learn the strength of the horses, to sit tighter than he has been
used to, and eventually to gallop his horse straight and fast. It
can often be two years or more before a lad actually gets a ride in
a race, but that first ride in public will be a moment he will never
forget.

Nicholson keeps four or five older, reliable horses especially
to provide his apprentices with experience of riding in public.
And, like most trainers, he keeps half of anything the youngster
earns in riding fees and percentages of winning prize money.
'I am in it to make a living', he says frankly. 'It's all a business.'
As the young apprentices improve, business can be given a
considerable boost by allowing them to ride for other trainers.
Apprentices are given a weight allowance of 7lb in all races
other than those confined to apprentices, until they have won
ten races; 5lb until their winners total fifty, and 3lb until they
reach the seventy-five mark. A really competent apprentice who
is still claiming an allowance can be a valuable asset, particularly
in a handicap, and once he has proved his worth there will be no
shortage of trainers competing for his services. Nicholson reckons
that a top-class apprentice can earn something like £5,000–
£6,000 by the time he is twenty-one, a figure that would be
much higher but for expenses and tax.

It is when a young jockey has lost his allowance that the testing
time comes. Many really promising apprentices have allowed
their success to go to their heads and found the going more and
more difficult once they had to compete on equal terms with their
senior colleagues. Some beset with weight problems turn to
the jumps, or quit racing altogether. But those who come through
their first couple of seasons as fully fledged jockeys with reasonable success are well on their way to top jockey status.

This happy status is achieved by only about one in two

thousand of the young hopefuls who originally sign on, however. The rest stay in the game as stable lads or drift out of racing altogether. Many nowadays leave for better-paid jobs in factories as soon as they realise they are not going to make the grade as jockeys. A training school for apprentices is organised at Great Bookham, near Leatherhead, in Surrey, with funds provided by the Levy Board, together with contributions from trainers with boys at the classes. Each course lasts six weeks and can cater for twelve apprentices, but by no means all trainers bother to take advantage of the facilities that are offered.

In the spring and summer of 1974 further courses financed by the Levy Board were launched at the National Equestrian Centre at Stoneleigh, in Warwickshire. The first, virtually identical to the apprentices course, was for girls aiming to become 'jockettes'; the other was essentially a course in riding and stable management aimed at school-leavers who might be interested in making racing their career but who came from basically non-riding backgrounds, as indeed a large proportion of jockeys do nowadays. The tutor is former jockey Johnnie Gilbert, assisted by instructors of the Equestrian Centre, and the students get free board and lodging during the six- to eight-week course, plus a small allowance. Those who complete a course successfully are offered a job with a racing trainer.

With their twin advantages of much more money and a central-ised racing system, the French go much further with their training scheme for young jockeys than Britain does, or even could. In France, apprentice jockeys combine formal work and lectures each afternoon with practical work with their individual trainers in the mornings. They are student jockeys for a year or more, and treated as students, not as sweated labour as is the case in the worst British yards. Apprentices have a much easier time of it in the United States, too, than in Britain. In the States they can learn their trade in a couple of years, and the facilities at their hostels, and the work they are expected to do, are incomparably better than is the case in Britain.

But given the difficulties, financial and otherwise, of the British racing scene, most would agree that the Levy Board and

Jockey Club were doing their best in this direction. Indeed, much of the criticism voiced about apprentice training—such as Tony Murray's much-publicised outburst at the Horserace Writers' Association annual Derby Awards luncheon in London in 1973—is criticism not so much of the scheme itself, but of the use owners and trainers make of it and the all too limited number of rides they give to apprentices. For instance, Murray, who had just accepted his award as 'Jockey of the Year', followed his description of the official scheme as 'a glorified pony club camp' by saying he would like to see trainers compelled to keep one horse for every twenty in their yard exclusively for apprentices. He thought the money spent by the Levy Board on the training scheme would be better spent on maintaining these horses and thereby giving young up and coming jockeys the chance to develop their skill by riding in public, which is the only way to learn the job of being a jockey.

Willie Carson, the cheeky-faced little Scotsman who deposed Lester Piggott as British champion in 1972 and seems set for a long reign at the top, is in no doubt about the importance of riding in public for an apprentice. 'It's the only way to learn the job,' he says, 'but all too few youngsters get the chance. I was lucky enough to be in the right place at the right time and got my break. For all I know there may be a dozen others as good as me who will never be heard of because they did not get the chances I did.'

There is no doubt that trainers and owners in Britain are curiously reluctant to entrust their horses to an apprentice in a race, however competent he has proved himself to be riding work on the gallops at home. If anything the situation seems even worse in Ireland. Leading commentator Michael O'Hehir, writing in the *Sporting Life* in November 1973, referred to the remarkable contrast between Ireland's lack of flat race riding talent and the stream of top-class National Hunt jockeys the country has produced: Pat Taaffe, Martin Molony, Willie Robinson, Ron Barry, Tommy Stack and countless others. Reminding his readers that although there had been five Irish-trained runners in the Prix de L'Arc de Triomphe that year, not one of them was ridden by an Irish jockey, O'Hehir went on:

> I feel that the dearth of Flat talent here traces to the fact that apprentices have been the forgotten work-things of the sport until recently. They have not had the consideration and, in many cases, the help and instruction, which should be theirs. . . . For so long apprentices have been the lads who 'did their two', got an occasional ride, and were then forgotten—a far from healthy situation.

What a contrast to the United States, where owners fall over themselves to grab a lad with any talent if he can still claim the magic 5lb allowance! But there are signs that the situation is improving even in Ireland, for the authorities there have recently launched a Racing Apprentice Centre of education in Dublin Road, Kildare, to provide their jockeys of the future with two-year courses in mathematics, crafts and civics as well as a veterinary course. Only a dozen lads could be accommodated in the original premises, but it is hoped to boost this to around sixty as soon as possible. And as a precaution against lads being regarded as 'forgotten work-things' in future, a new rule has been introduced which makes the first part of the apprenticeship a purely probationary period. At the end of it there is a three-way consultation between the lad and his parents, the trainer who employs him, and a representative of the Irish Turf Club to make sure that the decision on whether he stays in racing or leaves it is made in the best interests of the youngster concerned.

Most British jockeys will begin their working day at the crack of dawn, riding work for their retaining stables, or in the case of a freelance, at the request of a trainer who has booked him to partner the horse or horses concerned in some near-at-hand contest. After the morning session there is usually just time to snatch a hasty breakfast (if weight problems permit) before dashing off to the day's meeting, which can be anything up to two hundred miles away.

Before each race in which he has a ride, a jockey must 'weigh out' to make sure that his horse is carrying its correct weight according to the conditions of the race or the handicap. The

H

clerk of the scales records the weight as the jockey sits in the scales holding his saddle. (See plate, p 35.) If the weight is not enough, lumps of lead are inserted into pockets in the saddle cloth until the correct total is reached. If he finishes in the first four, the jockey must go through the same ritual after the race, too, although this time an allowance of a pound or two either side of the exact total is permitted to cover loss of weight during the race or extra poundage in the form of mud picked up en route. In most continental countries jockeys weigh out and in wearing their safety helmets for which an automatic allowance of $\frac{1}{2}$ kilo (about $1\frac{1}{4}$lb) is made, but in Britain the weight of the helmet is ignored.

About ten minutes before the race is due to start the jockeys troop out into the parade ring to meet up with their respective trainers and owners. If the jockey has not ridden the horse before the trainer may have detailed instructions for him, but in most cases the discussions that take place in the paddock are of a much more trivial nature. A likely source of last-minute information as to the horse's well being and peculiarities is the stable lad who is leading him round. Almost invariably the same lad looks after the horse at home and in many cases will know more about him than the trainer does.

Long before this stage, however, a thoughtful jockey will have worked out his own idea of how the race might go. Some horses will be known front-runners. They can be expected to make the early running at least. If it is a big race a fancied horse may have his own pacemaker in the field to ensure that the early pace is strong enough to ensure a truly run contest. Without either a front-runner or a pacemaker some middle and long distance races can become little more than sprints, with all the jockeys under orders to 'let the others make the pace' and all holding back until there is a concerted rush for the post in the last six or seven furlongs. In this kind of contest a horse who does not truly stay, for sake of example, $1\frac{1}{2}$ miles, might well win at such a distance. But as the 'race' was to all intents and purposes a sprint, the form is meaningless.

The ability to judge pace is one of the hallmarks of a great jockey, and one big reason why so many Australians go right to the top in European racing is because they are brought up on a diet of training gallops timed furlong by furlong so that they learn by instinct to judge accurately how fast a horse is going at all stages of the race. It does not necessarily matter where your horse is placed at any given moment (except at the post of course!) but it is essential to know how fast the race is being run, and how much reserve your mount is likely to have left.

For an example of timing *par excellence*, watch the film of the 1967 Derby, won by Lester Piggott on Sir Ivor, a horse who probably did not really stay the distance in fact, with a devastating swoop that looks too easy to be true. It was, of course, anything but easy. It is the hallmark of genius to make the difficult appear simple, and Piggott is a master of the art. Launched a few strides earlier, that same dramatic run would probably have petered out before the post arrived, leaving the stamina-packed Connaught the victor. A few strides later, and the post would have come too soon.

This ability to pace a race is even more vital when you are out in front. It is no good whatsoever dashing off like a bat out of hell if your mount is not capable of sustaining that sort of pace for the full distance of the race. On the other hand, races are often won in this manner by a horse capable of keeping up a strong relentless gallop and happy to race by himself—often at the expense of a better handicapped horse whose jockey has misjudged the pace and discovers too late that the leader is not going to 'come back to the field'.

Another art at which Piggott is supreme is that of 'waiting in front'—tactics which can be quite infuriating for his rivals, but sheer delight for the spectator. The maestro's mount grabs an early lead, but stays only a length or two ahead of the rest and simply spurts on again as soon as any of the others threaten to draw level. This is probably the hardest game of all to play, and it demands not only confidence and skill on the part of the jockey, but a horse capable of instant reaction to his rider's commands and capable of running his race in fits and starts. But when it comes off, there is nothing more effective. The 1962

Goodwood Cup was a spectacular example of how a race can be won against all the odds with these tactics in the right circumstances. Harry Carr and Sagacity played cat and mouse with Yves St Martin, on the hot favourite, Balto, who was undoubtedly a better horse, for the whole of the $2\frac{1}{4}$ miles and the jockey thoroughly deserved his share of the ovation they received when he and Sagacity reached the winner's enclosure.

When it comes to a sprint race, there is less chance for individual tactics, but the skill of the jockey is just as vital. A yard or two lost leaving the stalls would matter little in a race over ten furlongs, but over five, particularly on a fast course, it could be the difference between victory and defeat. It is important, therefore, for the jockey to be alert, and have his horse poised to leave the stalls the second they open, then to get his mount balanced and running into top speed in virtually the same movement. Balance is vital all through a sprint, of course, and by no means easy on a track such as Epsom. But of almost equal importance is to gallop straight—a jockey who doesn't could win only to lose the race in the stewards' room.

In the United States there is only one way to run a race—to go as fast as you can from start to finish. The 'waiting' race is virtually unheard of—and consequently very effective because of its element of surprise! An excellent example of the reverse situation —the orthodox American method working out magnificently in Britain—was the 1972 Benson and Hedges Stakes victory of Brazilian-born Braulio Baeza, who was flown across the Atlantic by trainer Vincent O'Brien to partner Roberto after Piggott, who had won the Derby on the colt two months earlier, chose to ride their narrowly defeated Epsom rival, Rheingold. Also in the field for the newly inaugurated York race was the hitherto undefeated Brigadier Gerard, and in the opinion of most critics Roberto, who had run badly in the Irish Sweeps Derby since his Epsom victory, would probably have to settle for third, or at the very best second place to the 'Brigadier'. Baeza, however, had other ideas. He swept Roberto out of the stalls American style, and romped home to a memorable victory. Brigadier Gerard, whose only defeat this turned out to be, could get no nearer to the Irish horse than a couple of lengths, and his defeat must be attributed largely to a masterly tactical ploy by O'Brien, executed to the letter by a very talented jockey.

The traditional waiting tactics are more often successful with horses racing over the longer distances favoured in Europe, however, although riding a waiting race need not be synonymous with being in last position. In the book, *Men and Horses I Have Known*, the late George Lambton describes Fred Archer thus: 'He was a marvel at the start . . . always well away. Even with a horse that he was going to wait with he was anxious to get well off, and to be in front in the first furlong.'

Archer, like Lester Piggott, knew that one could wait with a horse anywhere. There was no need to pull your mount to the back of the field if, by going easily and well within himself, you could remain up with the leaders. In fact just behind the leader is surely the best place to be unless you are riding a really hard puller who must be 'covered up' behind a wall of horses until you switch him out to make his challenge. For that race-winning run, when it comes, will last only so long, and it is surely obvious that ground lost for no good reason early in the race will be twice as hard to regain later on. The case is beautifully put by Mr Phil Bull's Timeform team in *Racehorses of 1973* when they state:

> The sight of a jockey checking his mount immediately after the start and hauling him to the rear of the field is a familiar one on our racecourses . . . To drop a horse out in the first half-furlong is simply to give the others start. The manoeuvre saves little energy in the horse; after the first hundred yards or so he has to race at the same pace as the leaders (if he is not to fall further behind) expending as much energy to do so as if he were lying upsides the leader or on his heels. And he still has to make up the ground sooner or later—probably later, when most of the runners are going along at, or at around, their top pace. More effort is required to make up five lengths in the last two furlongs than is saved by conceding five lengths in the first half furlong.

This masterly summing up should be indelibly imprinted on the mind of every aspiring young apprentice long before he gets to the point of riding in public.

Until 1972, only men were allowed to ride in races run under
Jockey Club rules, but in that year an experimental series of
races for women riders was held, and proved an enormous
success, both in terms of the races themselves and in the
attendances they attracted. Both the first two ladies' races, at
Kempton Park and Folkestone, were won by Meriel Tufnell,
who went on to become Britain's first lady champion, and
although the girls had their critics in the early days, the diehards
were pretty well silenced as the general standard of riding in
these races improved remarkably throughout the season. The
stewards of the Jockey Club were evidently impressed, for before
the second season of 'ladies-only' races was complete they had
announced a revolutionary plan to allow 'mixed' amateur races
in 1974, followed by permission for lady riders to apply for full
professional jockeys' licences for the 1975 season. (See plate,
p 72.)

The first 'mixed' race in Britain proved a real boost for the
girls. It was run at Nottingham on 1 April 1974 and the girls
really made 'April fools' of their male rivals. The winner was
Pee Mai, ridden by the 1973 lady champion, Linda Goodwill,
and they were followed home by two more girls, 'Babs' Stevens
and Jackie Thorne, with the first man finishing no nearer than
fourth.

Women jockeys are nothing new on the continent of Europe,
where they have been allowed for years in several countries,
including Norway, Austria and Holland, but even in these days
of Women's Lib few people dreamed that the all-male Jockey
Club would travel quite so far along the road to sex equality on
the Turf inside three short years! Even with this speed, however,
the Irish beat Britain to the post, for in January 1974 at Fairy-
house, Mrs Charmain Hill made history by becoming the first
woman rider in the British Isles to oppose the men on the flat.
Unfortunately for her, she could finish no nearer than third,
but this was in a field of twenty-two horses, twenty-one of them
ridden by men. And within a month the first female success had
been duly achieved, appropriately enough perhaps by Mrs
Rosemary Rooney, champion woman rider in Ireland the year

before. A £10,000 Levy Board scheme to train prospective women jockeys in Britain was announced early in 1974 and with increasing opportunities to gain race-riding experience a further improvement in standards must surely follow.

A jockey riding on the flat in Britain is paid £12 per race, from which £1.75 is deducted to go into an expense fund. He also gets £3.50 a day expenses, but out of this he makes a contribution of 10p a ride to the Levy Board insurance scheme, 5p to Jockeys Association funds, and pays valet fees which work out at close on £2 for the first two rides, plus an extra £1 for each ride after the first two and a couple of pounds on top for a winner. Then there is his equipment: a 2lb saddle costs about £50. Most jockeys have two or three of different sizes. Breeches are £9 a pair and riding boots between £20 and £30 a pair, with most jockeys getting through at least a couple of pairs in a year. Two skull caps, essential for racing and work riding, will set him back another tenner, and if he has weight problems, as many leading jockeys have, he will probably need his own sauna bath, which can cost anything up to £600. Some top jockeys' costs are increased further by having two complete sets of gear, one for the southern circuit, and one for when they race in the north.

Happily, however, jockeys do not have to hump their gear around with them all the time. The valets look after that. When he sets off for the races, master valet John Buckingham's car looks more like the stores wagon of a cavalry regiment than a gleaming 100mph saloon. Where the rear seats would be if he had room for them is piled high with saddles and other equipment. He can have up to fifty saddles, ranging in weight from the tiny two-pounders to bigger ones weighing anything up to 9lb. Then there are other items such as irons and leathers, girths, weight cloths, chafing pads and blinkers, breeches, boots, sweaters, skull caps and whips. Just about everything a jockey will need, in fact, except the colours of the owners for whom he will be riding. Bringing these silks to the course is the responsibility of the trainer.

These valets are a very important body of men, especially to a jockey with only a few short minutes in which to change his colours and collect a different saddle in between weighing in from one race and weighing out for the next. We described something of their work in *Over the Sticks*:

> The valets, who usually look after three or four jockeys each, work tremendously long hours caring for their jockeys' riding equipment. Often the valet has to be at the meeting by ten in the morning. On arrival, he proceeds to take out the saddles, which he will probably have carefully cleaned the previous night, and lays out the whole weighing room with tack. After racing he reverses the procedure, sponges and cleans the equipment ready for the next day. If it rains, the mud collected on the saddles and riding clothes will make his task even more difficult. At many meetings the valets, having arrived early in the morning, may not be able to leave until three hours or more after the last race. They accumulate tacks of their own over the years, often left to them by grateful jockeys on their retirement, and lend these to young apprentices, or those without a spare set. With Levy Board help, many courses have improved their accommodation and refreshment facilities for jockeys and valets, but at many smaller tracks they are all too often still faced with cramped, dingy weighing rooms, poor canteens, and nowhere to enjoy a quiet chat.

But if carrying the tools of his trade around is one chore most jockeys escape, travelling, at least in Britain, is something they simply cannot avoid. It is a fact long known to even the greenest insurance inspector, that jockeys not only drive fast cars, but almost always drive them harder and faster than any other type of motorist. In fact, it has been reliably estimated that the British jockey covers in a week the same mileage as an average motorist clocks up in a month. Few will get away with less than 30,000 miles of travelling a year, a costly as well as a tedious business.

With Britain's roads becoming ever more congested, more and more jockeys, especially from the main centres, are flying to meetings. It costs between £40–£50 an hour to hire a small plane, so if four jockeys and a couple of trainers get together to share one, the overall cost can work out very favourably compared to the cost of motoring. Peter Cadbury, chairman of Westward TV, and himself a keen racehorse owner, runs an air-taxi service used by many racing people, in conjunction with pilot Maurice Goor. They cut their overheads by housing the planes on the 800 acre Cadbury estate only a few miles from London's Heathrow airport, and operate flights to almost anywhere in Britain as well as to Ireland, France and Belgium. And they reckon their costs work out cheaper than hiring a car, almost as cheap as driving your own, and far quicker than either.

Whatever means of transport he uses, however, travelling is obviously a major problem for a jockey. Life and accident insurance used to be another, but a new scheme introduced in 1974 has done much to ease this particular worry. Taking a leaf out of the book of their Irish counterparts, who had introduced a similar plan a few months earlier, British racehorse owners agreed to finance a new scheme which more than doubled the compensation payable for both permanent and temporary disablement. Owners now pay £2 into a compensation fund each time they employ a jockey. The fund, administered by a board of trustees and a management committee which includes four jockeys, is used partly to insure all jockeys at Lloyds against permanent disablement, the rest of the money going to compensate temporarily disabled jockeys at a basic level of £35 per week, compared with £15 under the scheme which applied before. The maximum payment under the Lloyds policy is £15,000, compared to the previous £6,000.

Of course there are fewer injuries among flat race jockeys than with their National Hunt counterparts. But when an accident happens on the flat it tends to be serious, because of the speed at which the races are run. A jockey is hurtled down the Epsom five furlongs track, for example, in something like fifty-three or fifty-four seconds—that is an average of over 40mph. Falling off any object moving at that speed is unlikely to be an attractive experience, quite apart from the dangers from horses travelling immediately behind.

Jockey-turned-trainer Duncan Keith had two bad accidents in his riding days, almost exactly a year apart, and both caused by the same horse, London Melody, breaking a blood vessel. In the first crash, at Newbury, he broke nine major bones including the pelvis in four places, and two vertebrae, and was out for the rest of the season. A year later, almost to the day, the same thing happened at Lingfield Park when Keith was out in front in the jockeys' championship race with Joe Mercer. This time he broke his left arm and a thigh in two places. The horse was subsequently barred from racing. In 1972, promising apprentice Michael Kettle had a horrible smash at Newmarket when his mount suddenly ducked away at the point where the horses come off the open part of the course and the rails begin. Kettle's leg took the full force of the impact, but amazingly he was back in the saddle again and riding with all his old confidence before the end of the summer.

They were lucky compared with some. Twenty-one-year-old apprentice, Taffy Thomas, for instance, fractured his skull when his mount swerved after becoming unbalanced on a bend at Warwick, hurtling him against a concrete post. The tragedy was largely responsible for the introduction of skull caps to Britain.

But not all accidents on the flat happen during a race. With jockeys called upon to ride highly excitable young colts and fillies, who are sometimes having their very first experience of a racecourse and all the noise and sights and sounds associated with it, there are understandably some anxious moments in the parade ring and going down to the start. It was in the Ascot parade ring one black Saturday in September 1959 that leading jockey Manny Mercer, elder brother of Joe, was killed. His mount, Priddy Fair, reared, slipped and fell as they made their way from the paddock out on to the course. Mercer's head came into contact with a concrete post and he was also kicked in the face by the horse as she struggled to regain her feet. He was just twenty-nine.

In general, flat race jockeys do very well financially compared with their National Hunt counterparts. They are paid only £12 per ride, compared with a jump jockey's £15, and receive only 7.5 per cent of winning prize money as against 10 per cent. But they are riding for much bigger prizes so the percentage means a lot more, and although when there are accidents on the flat they tend to be nasty ones, by and large they run fewer risks.

The big difference between the two codes, however, is in the retainers available. Only a handful of the leading jump jockeys have retainers at all, but on the flat even a third-rater will have one, while the top boys can have as many as three, ranging from a few hundred a year for the third to several thousands for his principal retainer. A reasonably talented youngster just out of his apprenticeship could well have a retainer worth around £500–£600, while the number one rider for a powerful New-market stable could have earned something like £8,000 for the season before he rides a single horse. The terms of the agreement between trainer and jockey, incidentally, have to be approved by Weatherby's, and the money is paid to them on the jockey's behalf in two parts: one half before the season starts and the rest half-way through the year. The trainer then charges each of his owners a proportion of the sum involved according to the number of horses they have in his yard.

For the money, the jockey is naturally expected to ride for the stable at all times when required, and to get to know the horses in the string as well as possible, riding them regularly at exercise. The disadvantage of a retainer from the jockey's point of view is that he will sometimes be compelled to go to a meeting for one ride on an unfancied runner from his main retaining stable when he could have been on two or three likely winners for his second trainer at another meeting on the same day. But all things considered, and with most retainers the size they are, the system is probably weighted in his favour, for the money is, of course, over and above the basic riding fee, and quite separate from the large 'presents'—often in cash—paid by winning owners.

Trainers, too, benefit from the retainer system, since it is obviously better to have a top jockey available whenever you need him rather than have to take the chance of his being booked by a rival yard just when you have a horse right. It is also helpful on busy race days to have your horses ridden by a man who really knows them, rather than a stranger who needs to be told just about everything concerning each animal. So many things can happen so quickly before and during a race, and with a horse and rider who are accustomed to one another the chances of the right instinctive reaction in the split-second that may be all the time available are far greater than would otherwise be the case.

The retaining system is probably more widespread in Britain than elsewhere because there is more racing here, and because it is less centralised than in other countries. But the big French stables pay huge retainers, big enough to lure not only Australian stars like Bill Williamson, Bill Pyers and George Moore to France but in recent years British jockeys like Sandy Barclay and Jimmy Lindley, too.

The United States has something quite different: the jockey's agent. Unheard of at present in Britain—although there are signs that the day of his arrival may not be too far distant—the agent is as indispensable a part of an American jockey's equipment as his whip or saddle. In the specialisation-mad States, all a jockey has to do is ride races. There are full-time stable lads to do the stable work handled in Britain by apprentice jockeys; work-riders do almost all the exercise gallops. And as for the jockey or his wife sitting by the phone with the coming day or two's programmes before them, ringing up trainers to fix up rides, it is totally unheard of in the States. All the 'touting' is done for the jockey by his agent, who 'pushes' his man, arranges all his mounts, handles all the financial and travel arrangements, publicity and any outside perks . . . and happily collects his 10 per cent for his trouble.

As better communications and the lowering of international barriers continue to provide more and more opportunities for British jockeys in Europe and even further afield, more leading riders will probably follow the example of Lester Piggott and Eddie Hide and turn their backs on the comparative comfort of the retainer system in favour of the increased rewards of free-lancing at the very highest level. Already British jockeys can be seen practically every weekend riding in Germany, France, Italy and Scandinavia, and as the trend accelerates the time will soon come when an American-style agent is essential to handle the

complex business of travel arrangements, contacting foreign
trainers to confirm rides, and booking hotel accommodation.

But whatever American jockeys may lose financially in payments to their agents they more than make up again in what a
sociologist might term 'the quality of life'. Completely freed from
the need to worry about anything but riding his races, the jockey
in the States is also spared his British brother's wearisome
travelling, and enjoys sumptuous work conditions at the majority
of courses. Because of the American system of a long season of
six days a week racing at one centre, followed by a similar long
season at another, instead of two or three-day meetings scattered
all over the country, their jockeys need to travel only about once
every fifty days or so.

On race days, they will arrive at the course to start their
working day at around 11am. No crack-of-dawn turnout on the
Heath here! Morning gallops are left to the specialised work-
riders. But once a jockey has entered the racecourse weighing
room he will not be allowed out again, except to take part in his
races, until the day's racing is over. Not that he needs to go
anywhere, for this section of the course is more like a luxury
suite at the Hilton than the jockeys' quarters of any English track.
There is a viewing balcony with a good view over the course if
he wants to watch the racing; a TV room if he wants to forget it;
a canteen where he can put a few pounds on and a superb sauna
and rest room to sweat or sleep them off again.

For all this pampered luxury, however, the average American
jockey is not rated as highly as his British, Australian or French
counterpart, and one big reason for this must be the lack of variety
in American racing. Their jockeys get no experience of riding
different types of race on completely differing tracks as ours do,
because all American courses are pretty much the same. They
are all perfectly flat, all left-handed, and all sharp circuits of
about seven furlongs round. Not only that, but there is only one
style of racing: out of the stalls and the devil take the hind-
most! Lester Piggott caused an absolute uproar in the 1968
Washington International at Laurel Park by riding a perfect
waiting race to win on Sir Ivor in almost exactly the same way as

he had won the Epsom Derby on the same horse a few months previously. The American jockeys, and their racing press, virtually accused him of cheating. Piggott's reply was brief, to the point, and quite unprintable!

America's top jockey, a great admirer of Lester, incidentally, is a chirpy, 4ft 11in character from Texas called Willie Shoemaker who, at forty-two, has already ridden something like 6,500 winners. With a natural weight of 7st 2lb he obviously escapes the weight problems that beset so many of our leading jockeys, including Piggott, but it is interesting that he attributes a great deal of his success to a British-style start to his racing career, which included 'doing his two' as an apprentice would in England. Shoemaker told British journalist Jim Stanford, of the *Daily Mail* in an interview in 1973:

> I was apprenticed at fourteen to an old-style horse master in George Reeves, who insisted I did all the stable chores, just like your English boys. It was the greatest thing that happened to me, for I learned about horses, which is something many of the present set of younger American jockeys miss. They are jockeys, not horsemen. The English riders score because they know about the horse, and have a better understanding of horsemanship. I could still 'do my two' today if necessary, and I believe that is why horses run so kindly for me.

By no means everyone, even in Britain, would agree that our jockeys generally are the best in the world. In the opinion of many experts the statement might have been true in the period between the wars, when such men as Sir Gordon Richards, Steve Donoghue, Michael Beary, Harry Wragg, Joe Childs, Charlie Smirke, Rae Johnstone and many more were in their heyday, but is hardly justified today. These critics usually admit, albeit grudgingly, that Lester Piggott is in a class apart, although they often criticise his ultra-short riding style and rate him behind Sir Gordon as an all-round jockey. Almost inevitably they go on to criticise the rest of our top jockeys for being mesmerised by Piggott to the extent that they spend more time worrying about what he is doing than in riding their own race, and consequently allow him to dominate tactically almost any contest he chooses. It is a criticism which, if not invariably true, contains more than a grain of truth in it, as anyone who witnessed the 1972 St Leger at Doncaster, won by Piggott on Vincent O'Brien's colt, Boucher, will agree.

But significantly, the vast majority of racing's professionals will unhesitatingly name Piggott as the greatest living rider. Many will add that he is the best of all time. His style may upset the purists, but it is the privilege of genius to be unorthodox. Piggott possesses such superb balance that he can perch precariously on a paperweight saddle, his 'irons' pulled up ridiculously high, and still be capable of keeping his horse perfectly balanced and under control. It is those who imitate his style without possessing anything like his skill that deserve censure.

Former Royal jockey Harry Carr summed up the fellow professional colleague's view of Lester Piggott when he wrote: 'Piggott's a genius. He can inspire a horse to race above itself. He transfers his tremendous drive and will-to-win into the horse so that they think, move and fight as one. It's an unbeatable combination.'

It is not within the scope of this book to attempt either a detailed study of Piggott's character, or a comparison between him and other champion riders past and present. Many more qualified judges than ourselves have already done so, notably the former racing journalist Quintin Gilbey who, in the course of a memorable career, had witnessed and reported in both newspapers and books on the activities of at least three of the great jockeys of all time: Steve Donoghue, Sir Gordon Richards and Lester Piggott. For our own part, we will simply record that, in the view of most racing professionals, Piggott is the greatest of them all.

The worst feature of their chosen career for many jockeys is the constant battle to achieve a reasonable riding weight. The weight range in British races is from 7 stone to 10 stone, but no jockey could hope to ride at all regularly if he weighed much more than 8 stone. The result is that most of them have to live with one eye constantly on the scales. Fred Archer used to have a special mixture of his own, a purgative so powerful that a teaspoonful was reputed to be sufficient to turn most ordinary men 'inside out'. Present-day methods tend to be rather more scientific, and certainly less drastic, but the results of constant starvation and drug-assisted weight-reducing are still all too often very serious. Riding at his minimum weight at Newmarket a couple of years ago, Lester Piggott missed the small glass of water he allowed himself between races because he was involved in a stewards' inquiry. He collapsed from the effects of dehydration. The incident served to illustrate vividly the narrow safety margin a top jockey often allows himself, when he is determined to get down to his absolute minimum weight.

For Duncan Keith, winning jockey in seven hundred British races and over two hundred abroad, years of fighting a constant battle against nature suddenly became too much. In September 1972, he resigned his job as No 1 jockey to the powerful Peter Walwyn stable at Lambourn. 'For years I had been literally killing myself to keep my weight down', says Keith, whose stocky, 5ft 2in frame weighed just 8st 3lb on 1 September that year. By the middle of November, after just a couple of months' freedom from the unceasing battle to lose weight, he weighed 9st 8lb. His fifteen years of wasting have left him with a thyroid gland which no longer functions, and suffering from a form of sugar diabetes because of the misuse of pills which are designed to get rid of body fluid.

'Lots of overweight jockeys use these pills', says Keith. 'But after a while they no longer work. The body finds a way round them. In the end I could not get off more than 3lb, and I was never able to quench my thirst.' Towards the end of his riding career, Keith's life was dominated by pills and the sauna bath. Often he would have to get off 4lb between getting up and going to the races. It meant nothing but half a cup of black, unsweetened tea for breakfast followed by hours of sitting in the sauna bath. He would live on high-protein food like small steaks, chicken, fish and eggs with just a little wine, and occasionally champagne, to drink. After a while the stomach contracts and you don't want so much to eat. 'I had thirteen years of sweating it out in sauna baths three or four hours a day. It has put me off them for life', he says. 'My wife and family use our super-luxury sauna at home now, but not me. I have been scared to go anywhere near it since I gave up racing.'

Modern jockeys can be thankful for the sauna, however. In days gone by the methods of reducing one's weight in a hurry were far less pleasant. One erudite historian of the turf in the early 1800s, known simply as Taplin, wrote on the subject:

> If more than 4lb or 5lb reduction is required, additional purgation is needed by jockeys, together with abstention from food and drink, together with increased perspiration. Instances are numerous of jockeys wasting 14lb to 16lb in a short time when they have subjected themselves to the debilitating heat, fumes and steam immersed in a stable dung-hill for several hours.

Keith's ambition, like many jockeys when they retire, was to become a trainer, and happily he has now achieved his aim. In the autumn of 1972, Lester Piggott caused a flurry of premature retirement rumours by applying to his local council for planning permission to build stables on Hamilton Road at Newmarket. He was not planning to quit the saddle straight away but, canny as ever, he was aiming to make sure his stables were exactly as he wanted them by starting from scratch, and, as he pointed out, the longer he delayed the start of building, the more expensive his dream yard would become.

Although both Duncan Keith and Lester Piggott will no doubt join the sizeable band of men who have made the switch from riding to training with great success, for many jockeys this is not the answer. Some of them get jobs in stables when their riding careers end, but many unfortunately are lost to racing, so it is heartening to see that at least a few worthwhile jobs are being found for retired jockeys as racing officials. Gerry Scott and Bill Rees were made assistant starters in 1973 while other ex-jockeys, such as Bill Rickaby, have gone abroad to take up administrative posts in other countries. This is the reverse side of that swinging,

I

jet-set image referred to at the start of this chapter: the dedicated sportsman proud, in his later years, to have the chance to give back to racing something of his experience and skill in return for all that he has had out of the sport.

II

The Racing Year

On the flat, horses usually begin their careers as two-year-olds. There were once races for yearlings, but these were banned by the Jockey Club in 1859. Many people still have doubts about even two-year-olds taking part in the serious business of racing, for this is still very early in the average horse's development: the equivalent in human terms of a boy or girl in their early teens. The distances over which two-year-olds race is carefully controlled. In the early part of the season they are restricted to five furlongs. The Epsom Derby meeting in late May or early June is traditionally the time of the first two-year-old events over six furlongs. Later in the summer, races of seven furlongs and a mile are allowed and there are even one or two over a mile and a quarter in the final month of the season.

How often a horse races as a two-year-old will depend on many things: his size, his breeding, how good he is, and what country he happens to be racing in being just four of them. Size is important because if he is the tiny, sharp sort, his best, maybe his only, chance of winning is early on before his bigger and potentially better rivals appear on the scene. This is not to say that all small horses are necessarily hopeless. That would obviously be nonsense. After all, Mill Reef was no giant. But a small, none too well-bred animal can often win a race or two early in the season when he would not stand a chance later on, a good small horse can win whenever he chooses. At the other end of the scale to these 'early sorts' as trainers and racing journalists call them, are the big, gangling animals which rarely even look like racehorses until the late summer of their two-year-old days and sometimes do not even reach the racecourse until they are three.

The country in which a horse is racing makes a difference, too. British horses tend to race less often, especially as two-year-olds, than their French counterparts, and certainly less frequently than those in the United States. The difference becomes more marked the higher in class an animal is. In Britain and Ireland a two-year-old with any pretensions to running in the classics is raced very sparingly in his first season: three or four times on average, often less. Life is much tougher in the States, where survival of the fittest is regarded as the greatest of all racing mottos. Hail to Reason, the sire of Roberto, the 1972 Derby winner, who will always be remembered as the only horse ever to defeat Brigadier Gerard, ran eighteen times at the age of two, for example. Roberto himself, on the other hand, ran only four times. Nor do these figures tell the whole story. American racing is fiercely competitive. Not only does a horse have to be really fast to reach the top, he must be a hardy character, too, and this survival of the fittest attitude may well explain the current domination of top-class racing on both sides of the Atlantic by horses bred in the States.

Although there are many valuable and important prestige races for two-year-olds earlier in the season, particularly at Royal Ascot and Goodwood, it is from August onwards that the likely candidates for the following season's classic races really begin to sort themselves out. The historic Gimcrack Stakes, run over six furlongs at the big York festival in mid-August, is probably the first of these 'trials'. It is certainly the oldest, and carries with it a unique distinction. The 'Ancient Fraternitie' of the Gimcrack Club, founded in 1767 by the men who ran the York meetings in memory of a famous grey horse called Gimcrack who won no fewer than twenty-seven races in his career, hold their annual dinner in December. The owner of that year's Gimcrack Stakes winner is traditionally the guest of honour at the dinner, and makes the principal speech of the evening, usually dealing with some aspect of Turf politics.

After the Gimcrack there is the Champagne Stakes, over seven furlongs at Doncaster; the one-mile Royal Lodge Stakes at Ascot; three long-established Newmarket races: the Middle Park Stakes (six furlongs), Cheveley Park Stakes (six furlongs, fillies only) and the Dewhurst Stakes (seven furlongs); then the Horris Hill Stakes at Newbury over almost a mile before, in the final weeks of the season, the two most valuable events of their kind in Europe: the Observer Gold Cup at Doncaster and the Grand Criterium at Longchamps, in Paris, both run over a mile.

Until August all two-year-old races are non-handicaps, although there are several 'auction plates' where the runners are 'handicapped' according to the price at which they were sold at public auction. From August, however, there are a series of full handicaps for two-year-olds which have already won a race or have run at least three times. They are called, appropriately enough, nursery handicaps, but are anything but child's play either for the handicappers who must compile the weights or the punters trying to sort out the winner. There is usually very little public form at that stage on which to base one's opinion of a horse's merit, and there is the added complication that young horses, like young human beings, do not develop at a steady predictable rate, but in sudden spurts. Consequently, a two-year-old who was still a little backward in early July, meriting a low mark in a nursery, can often improve enough to make nonsense of the handicap mark by the middle of August, whereas another will still be virtually the same animal.

The most crucial period in the racing career of a top flat racehorse is his three-year-old season. The five classic races, which form the centrepiece of the flat in Britain, are for three-year-olds only, and if a horse is regarded as a future stallion much will depend on his performance in them. The first two classics, the 2,000 and 1,000 Guineas, are run over a mile at Newmarket in April; the Derby and the Oaks (1½ miles) at Epsom early in June, and the St Leger, the oldest of the quintet, over 1¾ miles at Doncaster in September. The 1,000 Guineas and the Oaks are confined to fillies, and in all the classics horses each carry 9 stone, except that fillies running against the colts in the three open races receive an allowance of 3lb. Entries for the first four classics, incidentally, close while the horses concerned are still two-year-olds.

Although there are now many valuable races in Europe, the Epsom Derby is still regarded by many as the supreme test of a thoroughbred, and success in the 'blue riband' of the British turf virtually guarantees a colt's reputation, and his value as a prospective stallion. Whether the Derby really deserves quite so high a regard is a matter of opinion. There are many who would argue that $1\frac{1}{2}$ miles over the twisty, undulating Epsom course is a unique, rather than supreme test of a racehorse, and that a fairer trial of merit by far is provided by two richly endowed events over the same distance open to three-year-olds and their elders: the King George VI and Queen Elizabeth Stakes at Ascot in July, and the most valuable race in Europe, the Prix de L'Arc de Triomphe, run at Longchamp, in October, and now regarded as the championship of Europe.

During their first season, as two-year-olds, most horses will compete only against other horses of the same age, although there are a few events, such as the Nunthorpe Stakes at York's big August meeting, and the Vernons Cup, now an established feature of the closing day of the flat season at Haydock Park, in which they can take on older horses. At three, the very best will still tend to be kept to races confined to those of their own age in the early part of the season, but by the mid-summer even the classic crop of the current season will be testing their strength against their counterparts of previous years that are still in training. The first such confrontation often comes in a race like the Eclipse Stakes at Sandown Park, and similar clashes are virtually assured in prestige international contests such as the King George VI and Queen Elizabeth Stakes, the Benson and Hedges Gold Cup at York, the Champion Stakes at Newmarket, and, of course, the 'Arc'.

The classics, and many of the other major races in the year, evolved more or less haphazardly into their present place in the scheme of things, but in recent years a great deal of thought has gone into planning the pattern of racing. In Britain, a committee was appointed in 1965 under the chairmanship of the Duke of Norfolk to study the subject, and the allied topic of prize money, and two years later a permanent Race Planning Committee, under Lord Porchester, took over to continue the work begun by their predecessors. More recently the racing authorities of Britain, Eire, France, Germany and Italy have started to produce a co-ordinated list of Pattern races, avoiding clashes wherever possible. The basic aim of the Pattern system is to provide a comprehensive series of races designed to test the best horses of various ages and over all kinds of distances, and to attempt to avoid overweighting the programme with one particular type of race. Britain stages around seventy Pattern races each season, graded into three groups according to either the value of the race or its international standing, and to qualify at all, a race must have at least £3,000 in prize money added to the stakes.

There will always be arguments about the exact details of the Pattern programme. Some critics will say there should be more money for long-distance events, others argue in favour of the classic mile and half as being the truest test, but few would disagree about the desirability of planning the season's programme, or, in these days of easier international travel, the need for the closest possible liaison with foreign racing authorities.

Many of Britain's Pattern races take place at the traditional festivals such as the Epsom Derby meeting, Royal Ascot, Goodwood, York, Doncaster and Ayr. These festivals, the longest of which lasts five days, are the nearest we come to the American system of centralised racing, and each has its own special atmosphere. Epsom on Derby Day, for example, is an incredible mixture of sights and sounds. Just across the track from the morning-dress elegance of the Members' Enclosure, out on the Downs in the centre of the course, are roundabouts and jellied-eel stalls, hurdy-gurdies, coconut shies and dodgem cars—all the fun of the fair.

You will not find a jellied-eel stall within half a mile of the most famous race meeting in the world, the four days of Royal Ascot in mid-June. Here the British flair for pageantry and spectacle combines with the British love of snobbery and social distinction to produce a sporting occasion that is quite unique. At the start of each day's programme members of the Royal family drive up the course in open carriages, while in the spacious, tree-shaded paddock, pop singers and merchant bankers, aristocrats and admirals mingle with film stars and model girls, dowagers and debutantes in a riot of colour and high fashion. It is such a heady mixture that all too often the cream of British thoroughbreds, racing for some of the richest prizes of the year, have to take second place, in the popular press at least, to the girl in the 'see-through' blouse, or the unofficial annual contest for who can wear the most outrageous headgear.

Goodwood, with its pleasant country estate atmosphere and breathtaking views over the Sussex downs, is altogether different again. For many it is the highlight of the racing year, possessing as it does many of Royal Ascot's best features, without its formality or much of its silliness. Blessed with a sunny day, and happily, Goodwood tends to be lucky in this respect, there can be few more pleasant race meetings than this, although northern racegoers will be quick to put forward the claims of their own festivals at York and Doncaster; especially the former, whose tremendously popular August meeting, highlighted by the historic two-year-old race for the Gimcrack Stakes and one of the biggest events of the season, the Ebor Handicap, goes a long way towards justifying York's description as the 'Ascot of the North'. In Yorkshire, by the way, they reverse this, claiming that Ascot should be called the 'York of the South', but that is typical Yorkshire pride for you. As a famous trainer from that county, Matthew Peacock, was in the habit of saying at the close of a meeting at Ascot or some other famous southern course: 'Cheerio. I am off back to England now.'

12

Racing Around the World

Racing is a truly international sport. It is nothing out of the ordinary nowadays for a British horse to run in Europe or in the United States, and vice versa, and racegoers are following suit. Indeed, with group air travel available at increasingly attractive rates, the foreign contingent at major international races such as France's Prix de L'Arc de Triomphe may soon outnumber the 'natives'. National racing authorities are increasingly working together. An owner can enter his horse for a race like the King George VI and Queen Elizabeth Stakes, for instance, in any of a dozen or more cities around the globe: Randwick, Australia; Brussels; Klampenborg, Denmark; Paris; Cologne; Dublin; Rome; Tokyo; Wellington, New Zealand; Oslo; Stockholm; New York and Moscow.

International competition undoubtedly stimulates interest and has been proved to increase betting turnover, so 'foreign raiders' are warmly welcomed in most countries. In London, the International Racing Bureau staff, headed by director David Hedges, encourage a two-way traffic, helping foreign owners and trainers coming to run their horses in Britain and handling entries of British horses bidding for foreign prizes. The Bureau operates a translation service to make sure the conditions of foreign races are understood and regularly publishes reminders of near at hand closing dates for entries in races abroad.

The metric scale is used for both race distances and weights in most countries, but this need present no problems to the British owner or racegoer, for a rough conversion of both is quick and easy. To convert metres into furlongs, for example, simply knock off the final two numbers and divide what is left by two. The result is the distance in furlongs. So a race over 1,000 metres is a five-furlong sprint (1,000, knock off 00=10÷2=5); one of 2,400 metres is approximately twelve furlongs, or one and a half miles. Weights in kilogrammes are slightly more difficult, but if you remember that 57 kilogrammes is 9 stone and that 1 kilogramme is 2·2lb you will not go far wrong. Somewhat surprisingly, races in the United States are still measured in furlongs, although Australia has gone metric, and with Britain's entry into the European Community it will probably not be very long before British racing is also using metres and kilogrammes.

It would be impossible to comment even briefly on every country where racing is a major sport, especially since their number is growing all the time. But these are some of the more important ones:

FRANCE

Although there are three hundred and sixty racecourses in France, almost all the racing of any importance takes place at a small cluster of courses around Paris: Longchamp, in the Bois de Boulogne; St Cloud; Maisons-Laffitte; Evry, a brand new course with computerised Tote which opened in February 1973; and Chantilly, which is also an important training centre. There is also a month of first-class racing at the Normandy seaside resort of Deauville in August, when there is usually a strong contingent of British-trained raiders. The country's remaining three hundred and fifty or so tracks mostly stage fewer than half a dozen days' racing each year.

Prize money generally is staggeringly high by British standards, and has risen in each of the last twelve years. This is one reason for the number of British horses racing in France and the large number of American-owned horses based there. The basis of this prosperity is the Tierce, a weekly pool bet based on a big race or particularly tricky handicap each Sunday. Punters have to select the first three horses in correct order, and it is extremely popular. There are no football pools in France, and consequently no Treble Chance, so this is the Frenchman's big jackpot bet.

Bookmakers are not allowed, but you can place bets on the Tote, including the Tierce, at Pari-Mutuel agencies (usually cafés) all over France, and these are then transmitted to a central organisation for inclusion in the pool. The French government takes some £153 million in tax from betting on racing each year, with a further £46 million going back to the sport in one way or another. Comparative figures for Britain, where the betting turnover is considerably bigger, are £63 million to the government and £5 million to racing.

Big races in France include the £165,000 Prix de L'Arc de Triomphe at Longchamp in October, which is the acknowledged championship of Europe and regularly attracts the world's greatest gathering of international horses, with top-class contestants from six or seven countries taking part. The Grand Prix de Paris at Longchamp and the Grand Prix de St Cloud in July are other major events, while among the other important races are the Grand Prix de Deauville, in August; the Prix du Cadran, France's equivalent of the Ascot Gold Cup, at Longchamp in May; and the French 'Derby and Oaks', the Prix du Jockey-Club and the Prix Diane, both at Chantilly in June.

UNITED STATES OF AMERICA

There are three major differences between racing in the United States and in Europe. Firstly, most American races are run on dirt, although turf racing is becoming increasingly popular. At Hollywood Park, for example, there are now often five turf races out of the eight or nine on the programme. The second difference is the similarity of the courses: they are all left-hand tracks between seven and eight furlongs round, and the first furlong is often run faster than the last, with horses going full pelt out of the stalls and slowing right down at the finish. Thirdly, there is the 'circus' style pattern to the sport in the States, with long seasons of intensive racing at one track followed by another season somewhere else. There are no training areas as such, all horses being stabled and trained at the track where they are to race, with trainers living in motels nearby for each course's season. A large track will have accommodation for 1,500 or 1,600 horses.

The average American racing programme would be monotonous in the extreme to many British racegoers. A typical nine-race card, for example, would feature half-a-dozen six-furlong races and one each over seven, eight and nine furlongs. Few American racegoers bother over-much with the horse's names: all betting is done by numbers.

It is impossible to mention anything like all the important American courses and races, but the main tracks in the New York area are Aqueduct and Belmont Park, both on Long Island, and Saratoga, one hundred miles to the north, where racing takes place during the holiday month of August, making it very much the American equivalent of Deauville. In New Jersey, there is a new track called Meadowlands, which is part of a two hundred million dollar sports complex which will include a baseball and boxing stadium.

The East Coast is well endowed with racecourses, including Atlantic City and Monmouth Park, as well as Laurel, home of the Washington DC International invitation race, run each November. The Washington arouses tremendous interest because of the international competition it provides, regularly bringing together champions from Europe, South America, Japan and Russia as well as the United States itself. There is also a course known as Garden State Park, near Philadelphia.

When racing closes down at these centres between December and March many of the horses, trainers and jockeys move down to California's Hollywood Park (Los Angeles) and Santa Anita tracks; to Gulfstream, Miami, or the beautiful Hialeah course, also in sunny Florida, where there are pink flamingoes on a lake in the middle of the course and palm trees around the paddock. Racing takes place almost all the year round, incidentally, at Chicago's Hawthorn Park racecourse.

Bookmakers are illegal in the States, although New York has

made a tentative experiment with betting shops on something like the British style. The Tote returns 85 per cent of turnover to winning punters, the remaining 15 per cent being split between the State (8 per cent) and the track (7 per cent).

Some of the top American races are the Washington DC International at Laurel Park, Maryland; and the American 'triple crown'; the Preakness Stakes at Pimlico, Maryland; the Belmont Stakes at Belmont Park, New York; and the Kentucky Derby at Churchill Downs, Louisville, Kentucky. Other big events include the Man O' War Stakes at Belmont Park, with £41,000 added money; Hollywood Gold Cup at Hollywood Park, Los Angeles (£72,000) and two major races for two-year-olds: the Garden State Stakes at Garden State Park, New Jersey (£52,000) and the Champagne Stakes at Belmont Park (£52,000).

JAPAN

The amount being spent by the Japanese on bloodstock—they accounted for almost half of the £2·4 million paid by foreign buyers at Tattersall's Newmarket Sales in 1973—is evidence of the fantastic growth of that country's racing industry in the last ten to fifteen years. The popularity of racing in Japan has to be seen to be believed. Crowds of over 100,000 at a Monday afternoon meeting are commonplace, while after 175,000 people had jammed the Fuchu course in Tokyo to see the 1962 Japanese Derby, police imposed a safety limit of 120,000 for the track. Now, intending spectators camp out for two or three nights beforehand to make sure of getting a place.

Racing is organised basically on the French pattern, with the five major courses clustered round Tokyo. Fuchu is one of these five, an oval track with a grass course of just over ten furlongs and a dirt course of one mile. Japanese tracks are run by local racecourse associations under the auspices of the Japan Racing Association. Betting is Tote only, and turnover has risen by 8 per cent in each of the past fifteen years.

For the racehorse owner, Japan in only one step this side of paradise. Unless his horse breaks a leg he can hardly fail to make money. Owners are paid to run their horses, and prize money is among the highest in the world. Not only that, but the trainer's and jockey's percentage is paid by the racecourse, not the owner.

Japan's horse-rearing area is on the North Island, Hokkaido. On the stud farms there you will find many former English horses, including Derby winners like Larkspur. In fact no fewer than sixteen Epsom Derby winners are now at stud in Japan. The country has not yet produced a horse of international standard itself, however, probably because the volcanic soil produces grass that is nowhere near so good for rearing horses as that grown on the limestone land of Kentucky, Ireland and Britain. The two biggest races of the year are the Spring and Autumn runnings of the Emperor's Plate, each worth about £45,000 to the winning owner.

WEST GERMANY

Although inevitably overshadowed to a certain extent by near-neighbour France, racing is becoming more and more important in West Germany because of increased prize money and an obvious desire to encourage international events. Total prize money in 1974 was around £3¼ million, and an increasing proportion of it is open to foreign horses.

The big three races, which all attract strong entries from other countries, are the Preis von Europa, run at Cologne in October and worth £54,000; the Preis von Baden, run at the Bavarian spa town of Baden-Baden in August, with the first prize of £34,000; and the £21,000 Grosser Preis von Nordrhein-Westfalen at Düsseldorf in July. But the German Derby, run at Hamburg in July, is confined to German-bred horses. Although not regarded as one of the top countries for bloodstock, West Germany occasionally produces a first-class horse. Lombard, one of Europe's best middle-distance horses in 1972, is one example.

The principal courses are those at Cologne, Düsseldorf and Hamburg, although there are many lesser tracks in addition. There are both bookmakers and Tote on the course, and the Renquintet, a forecast bet on the lines of the French Tierce, is becoming increasingly popular. For this, contestants have to forecast the first five in a selected race each Sunday.

ITALY

Racing is not a major sport in Italy, although prize money per head of horse is among the best in the world. There are not all that many horses in training in Italy, and fields are usually small by British and French standards, with the result that each horse has that much more chance of finishing in the money.

The San Siro course at Milan is one of the best racecourses in the world: a flat, testing track with a four-furlong run-in. The Italian Derby and other classics are run at the Campanella course in Rome, and there is also racing regularly at Turin and Naples. Betting is mainly Tote, but there are bookmakers on the course.

In winter, most Italian racehorses are moved to Pisa, where the climate is milder than in Milan and where there are wonderful, sand-based gallops. It was to Pisa that Irish trainer Vincent O'Brien sent Sir Ivor to spend the winter before his 2,000 Guineas and Derby triumphs of 1968.

Curiously enough, although Italy is not a great racing nation, and tends to fight shy of international competition, the country produced the horse reckoned by many expert judges to be among the three best, if not *the* best of this century—Ribot. Foaled in 1952, Ribot was bred by the Razza Dormello-Olgiata and retired undefeated after sixteen races, a record that not even Brigadier Gerard managed to beat. Ribot's victories included the Prix de L'Arc de Triomphe (twice) and the King George VI and Queen Elizabeth Stakes at Ascot, while among several top-class horses sired by him are two more 'Arc' winners in Molvedo and Prince Royal II, and British classic winners Ragusa, Ribocco, Ribero and Long Look.

AUSTRALIA AND NEW ZEALAND

Racing is more than a mere sport in Australia. It is a way of life. The Australians are natural gamblers, and the talk in any bar or hotel will usually revolve around the day's racing. Many of the commercial radio stations will devote a whole hour a day to racing, with news and interviews with jockeys and trainers as well as results and commentaries.

The major racing is staged at the big city tracks of Melbourne, Sydney, Brisbane, Adelaide and Perth, although in midweek there are plenty of country, or 'picnic' meetings on the other fifty or more smaller tracks. The biggest race by far is the Melbourne Cup, which attracts tremendous interest all over Australia, with practically everyone having a bet on it.

Bookmakers are allowed in Australia, but only on the course. There are Tote betting shops and Tote credit facilities for telephone bets, all fed into an efficient, computerised Tote. The Totalisator Agency Board deducts 7·5 per cent from the Tote pool for distribution as prize money and for other purposes, with the state government taking 5·5 per cent. Attendances are high, and betting turnover is increasing, as is prize money.

New Zealand is important as a breeding area for Australia, and increasingly nowadays, Japan. Australian and Japanese owners and trainers flock to yearling sales such as those at Trentham, Wellington, and usually buy something like three out of every four horses that come up for sale. Many of them are sired by English horses that have been exported to New Zealand. Of the eighteen winners of the Melbourne Cup to 1972 inclusive, no fewer than thirteen were bred in New Zealand.

BELGIUM

Conscious of the tourist potential of racing, apart from the stimulus international competition gives to the betting turnover, Belgium began a campaign through the International Racing Bureau in 1969 to attract runners to their July and August holiday meetings at Ostend. The result has been remarkable. From three or four British runners four years ago they now have eighty or more, including a regular contingent from the David Robinson stables. Prize money is high for the standard of racing, and the Ostend track, facing the beach, is a delightful spot on a sunny day. Indeed, regular parties of British racegoers now visit Ostend on day excursions from London, Southend and Dover to enjoy racing on a summer Sunday.

Bookmakers are allowed on the course in Belgium and there is also an efficient Tote. Many of the runners come from Holland and Germany as well as Belgium.

NORWAY

Norway is another country which actively encourages foreign-trained runners. Virtually all the flat racing takes place at the attractive Ovrevoll course just outside Oslo. Prize money is not outstandingly high, but generous travel allowances are paid for certain races and top British jockeys like Tony Murray, Willie Carson and Eddie Hide are often seen in action at the Sunday meetings. In 1970, Epsom-trained Happy Hunter won the Norwegian Derby and St Leger, and a year later Royal Park, from Newmarket, won the St Leger.

There are no bookmakers in Norway, and all betting is on the Tote. As in many European countries, punters seem to be keener on forecast and 'triple' betting (placing the first three in correct order) than in straight win and place bets. On the Norwegian Grand National and St Leger Day in October there is a ten-race programme featuring two jackpots. Women jockeys have been permitted for many years, and compete against men.

The Norwegian Jockey Club estimated the annual cost of maintaining a horse in training at £1,150 in 1973, but one in four of the country's racehorses are reckoned to earn their keep from prize money.

SOVIET UNION

Like everything else in the Soviet Union, racing is run by the State, through a government director of racing. There are no owners, and no prize money, but the stud which produced the winner of a race is awarded a number of points, and at the end of the season these are totalled up and converted into tokens

K

which may be used by the members of the stud farm to buy items in the shops. There is only a limited amount of betting, all on the Tote. Russia has produced some good international horses, and often has a runner in the Washington International race. Their best in recent years was Anilin, who competed in the Preis von Europa three times.

HUNGARY

Once one of the major racing countries in the world—ranked in fourth place at the start of the century—Hungary was virtually put out of existence as a racing nation by World War II, during which the Russians and Germans confiscated most of the best bloodstock. It was a blow from which the sport has never recovered, and such racing as there is today is of very minor importance.

A study of Hungarian racing history, however, shows there is nothing new in the idea of international competition. A mare called Kincsem, bred in Hungary, raced all over Europe in the years 1876–9 and retired unbeaten in fifty-four races, her successes including the Grand Prix de Deauville, the Goodwood Cup and the Grosser Preis von Baden, which she won no less than three times. There were no aeroplanes in those days, of course, so all Kincsem's travelling was done by train. Luckily she loved this means of transport, and went everywhere quite contentedly, provided she was accompanied by her closest friend, a cat.

HOLLAND

Flat racing in Holland takes second place to harness racing, or trotting, but there are signs of increasing interest, and attendances at the twice-weekly mixed trotting and flat meetings at the beautiful Duindigt course in The Hague are increasing. The racecourse is superbly appointed, with computerised Tote and an elegant restaurant complete with luxury piled carpets, and even chandeliers.

All the classics, and many other valuable races are confined to horses bred in Holland, but there is increasing international competition, particularly in the amateur riders' events. Professional women jockeys have been allowed since 1966, and compete on equal terms with men. In fact the 1971 Netherlands Derby was won by a woman jockey.

Thanks to a powerful anti-gambling lobby in parliament, there is no off-course betting whatsoever in Holland, and no bookmakers are allowed. All horses are placed in three grades, and for handicap races may compete only in their own grade or higher. A central handicap showing a horse's current grading and his exact handicap mark is published each month by the Dutch Jockey Club, who publish twice-weekly a magazine which acts as official racecard for all meetings as well as publicising the sport and recording official decisions.

SPAIN

The Spanish Ministry of Tourism is currently investing £2,000,000 in racing in an attempt to attract British-trained horses from the second and third grades to race in Spain. There were fewer than three hundred racehorses in Spain at the start of 1973 but with prize money averaging around £850 a race, the Spanish Jockey Club estimate that almost half of them at least recovered the £600 a year it costs to keep them in training, and that most of these made a profit from prize money.

Fig 5   Locations of flat-racing courses in Great Britain

13

Racecourses of Great Britain and Ireland

ASCOT

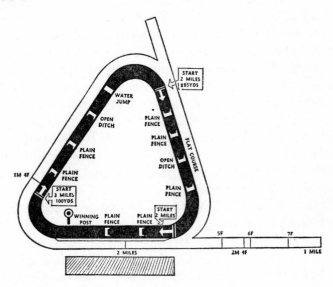

The only racecourse in Britain owned by the Crown, Ascot owes its place in racing history to Queen Anne, who thought it looked a good place for a meeting as she drove across the Heath one day in 1711. Today's course was reconstructed in 1955, and consists of an oval track of just over one and three-quarter miles, joined by the straight Hunt Cup course, a mile long, two and a half furlongs from the winning post. It is a testing course, for the last seven furlongs are uphill and in races on the round course a horse must be handily placed approaching the final bend to be in with a chance because of the short run-in. The draw has no significant effect at Ascot.

Large modern stands, with heating and escalators, make for comfortable viewing, although the main stand is badly angled for judging a close finish. At all except the big summer meetings the paddock is in front of the main stands; otherwise it is a long walk, including a stretch of underground tunnel, from all enclosures but the Royal enclosure.

The principal meeting is the four-day Royal Ascot festival in mid-June which invariably attracts almost all the top horses in Britain and many from abroad. Each day's programme begins with a procession in which the Royal family drive up the course in open carriages. Traditional opening race of Royal Ascot is the Queen Anne Stakes, in honour of the course's founder, and of the many other notable races the biggest prestige event is probably the Ascot Gold Cup, first run in 1807. The Royal Hunt Cup, over a mile, on the Wednesday of the Royal meeting, is one of the biggest betting races of the year. It was first run in 1843.

The one-and-a-half-mile King George VI and Queen Elizabeth Stakes, which takes place at the July meeting, is one of the most valuable and important races in Europe and always attracts a field of the highest calibre.

A word of warning. If you wish to apply for a voucher for the Royal enclosure at the Royal Ascot meeting, you should do so during March and April to Her Majesty's Representative, Ascot Office, St James's Palace, London SW1. First-time applicants will be asked to complete a form and have it signed by a sponsor. Visitors from abroad should apply through their representative Ambassadors or High Commissioners, or through the Commonwealth Office in London.

AYR

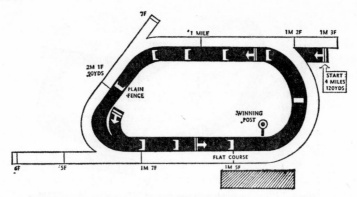

One of the best and fairest courses in Great Britain, and certainly the finest in Scotland, Ayr leaves it late to stage the highlight of its year, the four-day Western meeting in September. This has been a regular attraction for owners and racegoers from all parts of the country since the 1820s. Its principal race, the six furlong Ayr Gold Cup, was once confined to Scottish-bred horses, but now unfailingly draws the best sprinters in the land and invariably produces an exciting contest.

The course is left-handed and just over one and a half miles round with a run-in of about half a mile. There is a straight six furlongs, and because of the sandy sub-soil the whole track is very quick-drying, making for good going almost all the year round. The bends are well banked and easy and the course is almost entirely flat. The draw favours high numbers over five and six furlongs, with low numbers best on the round course.

BATH

Bath, where racing was first recorded in 1728, is the highest flat-racing course in Britain, a factor that may account for some of the odd results that are a feature here. The track itself is tricky, although the camber on the bend into the straight has been impoved, and jockeyship is important when considering the chances of your fancy. Both horses and jockeys with a good

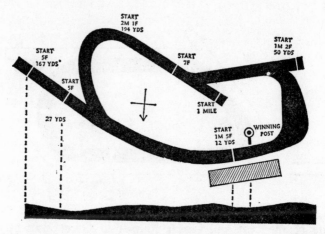

record on the course are worth following. The oval track is left-handed and just over one and a half miles round, with a straight run-in of half a mile, mostly uphill. Because of the old downland turf on which the track is laid out, the going is almost always good, even in dry weather. The draw favours low numbers in races of up to a mile.

BEVERLEY

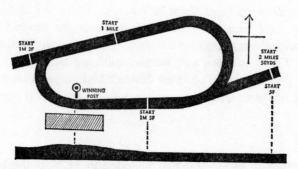

Far from being the classiest course in the north, this friendly little East Yorkshire meeting is nevertheless thriving on a policy of catering for the family. From the horse's point of view it is anything but cosy. Its broad, flat, oval track, right-handed, and just over one and a half miles round, has a straight run-in of

half a mile and presents a very stern test of stamina. So before
you back anything here you should make quite certain the animal
will stay the full trip and a little bit more. Two-year-old races
at Beverley are notoriously trappy, although two of the top events
run here are for that age group: the Hilary Needler Trophy (for
fillies only) and the R. B. Massey Trophy, both run over five
furlongs in June. The Charles Elsey Challenge Trophy, at the
May meeting, honours the memory of one of the most famous
of Yorkshire trainers.

The draw at Beverley favours high numbers over five and six
furlongs.

BRIGHTON

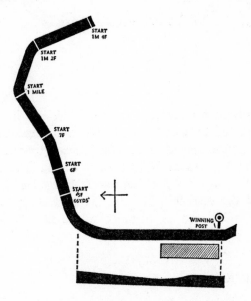

Brighton is one of the more popular, if not among the most
elegant of British racecourses, enjoying a breezy position high on
a hill overlooking the famous resort, with a view of the sea. The
track is an easy, undulating left-hand sweep in the shape of a
horseshoe, just one and a half miles long: no race of more than
this distance is run here. In many respects it is similar to Epsom,

and horses that do well on that course, especially two-year-olds, generally do well here, too. Jockeyship is very important, and so is a low draw in sprint races.

CARLISLE

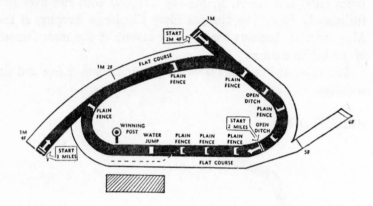

An unpretentious northern course, Carlisle is in a beautiful setting with the Lakeland hills providing the backcloth. Right-handed and pear-shaped, the course is just over one and a half miles round and testing in character. Racing here has a long history, with two of the oldest events being run at the main meeting of the year, in July: the Cumberland Plate, over one and a half miles, and the historic Carlisle Bell, over one mile. High numbers are best in the draw.

CATTERICK

With memories dominated by Catterick's army-camp image, most people are surprised to see, either 'live' or via television, what a pretty place this enterprising little Yorkshire course is. Racing has been held here since 1783 and in recent years great improvements have been made for spectators and to improve the quality of racing. The course is well situated, adjacent to the main A1.

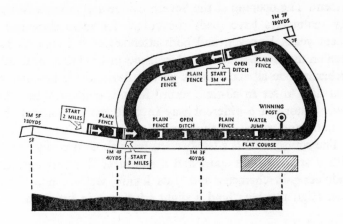

Catterick is a sharp, undulating, left-hand course, little more than a mile round, and is an ideal track for the nippy type of horse who is fast from the gate, or a confirmed front runner. The big, long-striding animal is at a distinct disadvantage. Low numbers are favoured in the draw.

CHEPSTOW

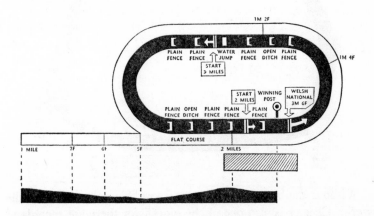

The newest racecourse in Britain, built only in 1926, Chepstow stages more distinguished National Hunt racing than flat at present. The opening of the Severn Bridge and the new M4 and M5 motorways have made the course far more accessible in recent years, however, and both attendances and runners have been on the increase. It was at Chepstow in 1933 that Sir Gordon Richards rode all six winners on one day and the first five the next day, to set an all-time record for this country. The course made history in a different way in 1970 when it staged show jumping and racing on the same afternoon.

The course itself is a left-handed track about two miles round, with a straight mile spur, and a run-in of five furlongs. It is undulating in character and suits handy, well-balanced horses best. High numbers hold a slight advantage in the draw.

CHESTER

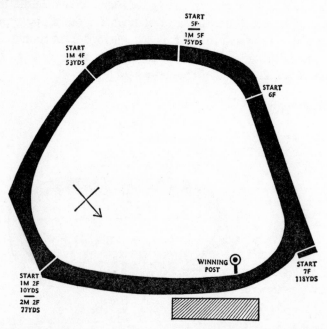

Without doubt one of the most incredible racecourses in the world, Chester is also one of the oldest, for there are records of meetings on the Roodeye, by the River Dee, in 1540. The circular course is barely a mile round, and left-handed, with the ancient city wall, built by the Romans, alongside the run-in, which is only 230yd long—by far the shortest of any British track. Because of its peculiarities, racing at Chester has a quality all of its own. In long-distance races the horses are almost continuously on the turn, while sprints are invariably extremely exciting. It is a positive disadvantage to be drawn in anything but the low numbers in a sprint and small, well-balanced horses naturally tend to do best.

Until recently there was only one meeting a year, but there are now two-day meetings in July and August as well as the principal fixture in early May, at which the time-honoured Chester Cup, a two and a quarter mile handicap first run in 1824, is the highlight of the second day. Another feature race is the one and a half mile Chester Vase, usually regarded as a significant trial for the Derby. Many of its winners have gone on to success in the premier classic, including Papyrus, Hyperion, Windsor Lad, Tulyar and Parthia.

DONCASTER

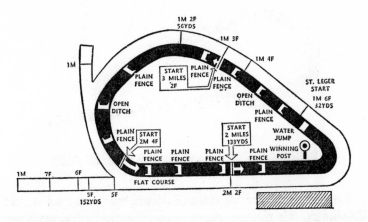

One of Britain's great racecourses, Doncaster is handily situated for both the A1 and M1, and is famous above all else as the home of the St Leger, the oldest of the five classic races for three-year-olds, and inaugurated in 1776. The St Leger, the climax of the four-day September meeting, the most important of the season, is run over a distance of one mile, six furlongs and one hundred and thirty-two yards, just under a complete circuit of the pear-shaped, left-handed course. A sweeping turn leads into a run-in of four and a half furlongs, and there is a broad, flat straight mile which gives every chance to the out-and-out galloper. Mile races are also run on the round course. The draw favours high numbers in races on the straight course.

As well as the final classic, there are several other important races run at Doncaster, which now has a magnificent new grand-stand with the paddock situated in front of it. The course stages the first meeting of the British flat-racing season each March, with the Lincolnshire Handicap, over the straight mile, on the Saturday. Towards the end of the season, there is the Observer Gold Cup, one of the most valuable two-year-old events in Europe, and generally a reliable guide to the following season's classics.

EDINBURGH

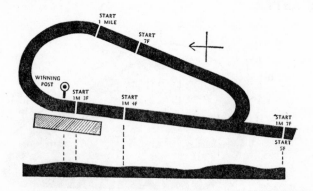

Situated at the seaside town of Musselburgh, five miles from Edinburgh, this modest course faced extinction a few years ago, but was saved mainly through the efforts of the late Lord Rosebery. The oval track is left-handed, and about one and a quarter miles round, with sharp bends and a run-in of approxi-mately half a mile. There is a straight five-furlong course. Edinburgh is essentially a course for the handy horse, and fast starters do well in the sprints. The draw favours high numbers in races over seven furlongs and a mile.

EPSOM

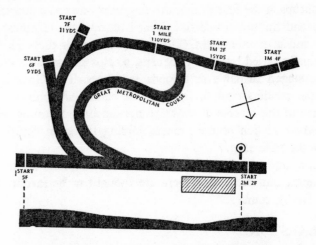

Thanks to the Derby, first run here in 1780, the one and a half mile Epsom track is world famous. It makes considerable demands on a horse, who needs to be adaptable enough to handle the sharp turns, well balanced enough to cope with the gradients and undulations of the track, and in addition possess the stamina for the long uphill start and the punishing final hill, only a matter of yards from the winning post. Races on the Derby course are run anti-clockwise and there are spurs off the main track for six-furlong and seven-furlong races. The run in from Tattenham Corner, which, incidentally has its own railway station, is under four furlongs, so a horse needs to be handily placed at this point if he is to have much chance of winning. The adjoining five-furlong course is one of the fastest in the world, with a violent downhill run for the first couple of furlongs.

Naturally, small, well-balanced horses do best at Epsom, especially in sprints, although jockeyship is almost as important. It is no coincidence that Lester Piggott has so many winners here. The only jockey to match his success rate in the Derby was Steve Donoghue who won the classic six times, including three years in succession. The Oaks, the fillies' classic over the Derby distance of one and a half miles, is run at the same June meeting and other important races here include the one and a half mile Coronation Cup, also at the June meeting, and two historic handicaps at the first Spring meeting: the one and a quarter mile City and Suburban and the Great Metropolitan Handicap, over two and a quarter miles. The prize money for these races was originally raised by local publicans, so Epsom can fairly claim to have staged Britain's first sponsored races. The Great Metropolitan runners start in front of the stands and run down the course in the reverse direction to normal before turning off on a roped-off section of the Downs, joining the main course again near the mile start.

Low numbers are best in the draw at Epsom up to seven furlongs, but middle numbers are thought to be favoured over the Derby course.

FOLKESTONE

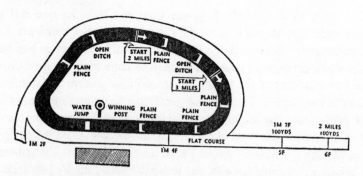

An attractive little course, actually situated not in Folkestone itself but eight miles away at Westenhanger, on the main rail line to London and beside the A20 road. After facing extinction a few years ago the course has picked up a great deal in recent seasons, and when the Channel Tunnel is eventually completed it could become as popular with day-trippers from France and Belgium as it is already with British holidaymakers. The track is right-handed, about one mile three furlongs round, with a run-in of three and a half furlongs. It is mostly undulating, and regarded as a fairly easy track, where adaptability counts for more than stamina. Low numbers are favoured by the draw in races on the straight six-furlongs course. The children's playground at Folkestone, incidentally, features a galleon in addition to the usual roundabouts and swings.

GOODWOOD

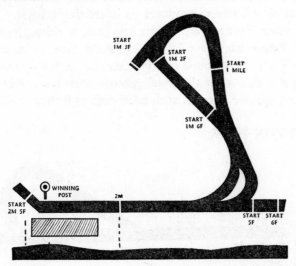

One of the loveliest racecourses in Europe, Goodwood is laid out in the grounds of the Duke of Richmond's estate, five miles from Chichester, in Sussex. There is a delightful informality about its big summer meeting, which for many racegoers is the highspot of the whole season, while the view over the Downs from the top of the Grandstand is quite breathtaking. The first meeting here was held by members of the Goodwood Hunt and the Sussex militia in 1801, but the rapid development of the course was largely due to the enthusiasm of Lord George Bentinck, who for many years had his horses trained here.

The track itself is undulating and on the whole easy, basically right-handed but including left-hand turns as well in long-distance events (see plan). High numbers are favoured by the draw in sprint races.

L

The summer festival is packed with important races, but among the most popular are the six furlongs Stewards Cup, which invariably attracts heavy ante-post betting, and the high-class Sussex Stakes, over a mile. There is also a £10,000 handicap, currently sponsored by the Extel Company, over one and a quarter miles and the time-honoured Goodwood Cup, a two miles five furlongs stamina test which rarely attracts a large field but almost always produces an interesting contest.

The other meetings are of less importance, although the late August fixture has the £5,000 Goodwood Mile as its feature. The children's playground on this course is worth a mention, for as well as facilities for the usual outdoor activities, children can also enjoy quieter pursuits such as modelling if they prefer.

HAMILTON PARK

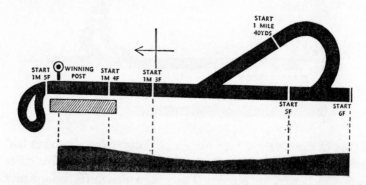

This popular Scottish course, just eleven miles from Glasgow, pioneered evening racing in 1947, and was also the first to try a morning meeting. They started at 11am on Cup Final day in 1971. There was racing in the district as early as the 1780s but the present course was laid out between 1887 and 1890 in response to a request from a group of Glasgow sportsmen.

Basically, Hamilton is a straight six-furlong stretch with a loop at one end, so its shape resembles that of a tennis racquet. For races over one mile five furlongs, horses start in front of the stands, run down the course, round the loop and back up the straight again. A famous feature is a pronounced dip about three furlongs from home which has caught out many a fancied runner. The finish is uphill, too, so it is not an easy course. Middle and high numbers are favoured in the draw.

HAYDOCK PARK

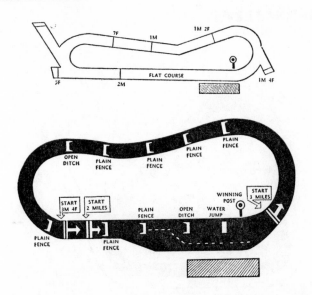

Under the direction of a bright, go-ahead executive, Haydock has made rapid progress in the last decade, and is now one of the principal courses in the North. Situated close to the M6 motorway, and with the huge Lancashire conurbation to draw upon for attendances, an even brighter future seems assured. The left-handed, undulating track is one mile and five furlongs round with just one right-hand turn just over a mile from home. The straight five furlongs and the six furlong and one and a half mile courses all start on spurs from the main circuit. Although basically an easy course, the last half a mile is uphill and a horse needs to be able to stay the full distance of his race. Low numbers are slightly favoured by the draw in races over six and seven furlongs.

The amenities do not as yet quite match up to the high quality of the racing, but no doubt this will change, and there is a splendid new Newton Stand which serves the old cheap ring, too.

Haydock has the distinction of staging the closing fixture of the British flat season each November, when the feature race is the Vernons Sprint, sponsored by the pools firm which has its headquarters at nearby Liverpool.

KEMPTON PARK

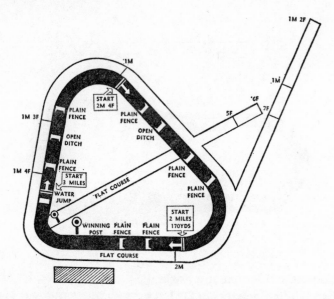

Set in three hundred acres of what used to be magnificent parkland, Kempton has never really managed to attract regularly the sort of crowds the generally high standard of its racing deserves —despite its proximity to London. Perhaps the completion of the M3 motorway, which is to pass nearby, will help in this respect. The course, at Sunbury-on-Thames, fourteen miles from the centre of London, is right-handed, triangular and just over one mile and five furlongs round. A separate five-furlong course cuts across the centre. Both tracks are almost completely flat, and the draw has little significant effect.

Kempton was the venue for Britain's first ladies' race under Jockey Club rules, run in May 1972, and won by Meriel Tufnell on Scorched Earth. Miss Tufnell went on to become the first lady champion. Kempton's principal meeting is usually on the Saturday and Monday of Easter weekend, when the feature races include the 2,000 and 1,000 Guineas Trials and the Easter Monday stayers' race, the Queen's Prize. The one and a quarter mile Jubilee Handicap is another big event run here. Amenities are rapidly being improved, and there is a beautiful new restaurant, the Kempton Manor, in the Tattersalls and Members enclosure.

LANARK

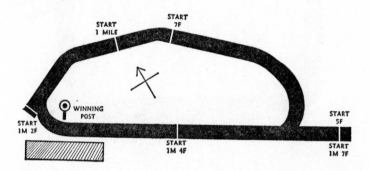

Set amid some superb Scottish scenery, Lanark has the honour of staging the oldest race in Britain, the Lanark Silver Bell, which was instituted by King William the Lion of Scotland in the twelfth century. It is a right-handed track, some one and a quarter miles round, with easy turns and a half-mile run-in. But for all this it is not a track for galloping types. The draw favours high numbers on the round course, low numbers in sprints.

LEICESTER

Far from being one of Britain's lovelier racecourses, Leicester nevertheless stages some interesting racing, and the efficient watering system, one of the first of its kind to be installed on a British course, virtually ensures reasonable going in even the

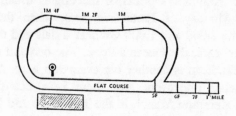

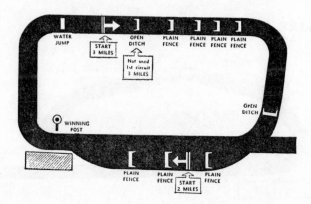

driest spells. The main track is a right-handed, undulating circuit, nearly two miles round, with a stiff uphill run-in of over half a mile. It is essentially a galloping course, and presents a very stern test for two-year-olds, hence the frequent form upsets in this age group. There is also a straight mile, one of the few in Britain. Low numbers are favoured by the draw in sprints, but it has little effect otherwise.

LINGFIELD PARK

Known as 'Lovely Lingfield' this Surrey course has a strong similarity to Epsom, so not surprisingly its principal race is the one and a half mile Lingfield Derby Trial in May, which has been won by several horses, including Tulyar and Parthia, who went on to victory in the 'Blue Riband'. Its left-handed circuit is roughly one and a quarter miles round, slightly smaller than

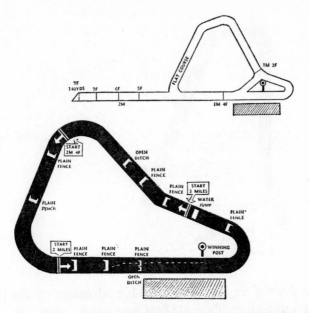

Epsom, but has a similar climb followed by a downhill run into a sweeping turn into the straight, which is just under half a mile in length. There is also a straight course about half a furlong short of a mile, and downhill all the way, so speed and a good action are all-important here.

The draw is thought to favour high numbers generally on the straight course, although in heavy going the advantage is strongly in favour of the low numbers.

LIVERPOOL (Aintree)

Flat racing comes a poor second to steeplechasing at this famous jumping course, although sponsorship has done something to improve matters at the two mixed meetings held here each year. The future of the course is still in the balance, and until it is finally decided little is likely to be done about the atrocious amenities—or rather, lack of them. The flat-racing track is a left-handed oval of approximately one and a quarter miles, with a separate five-furlongs course across the centre.

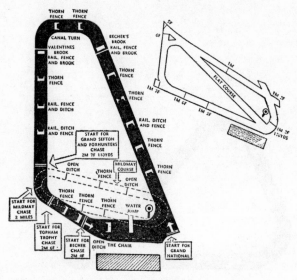

The draw gives low numbers a big advantage on the round course, but high numbers are best over five furlongs.

NEWBURY

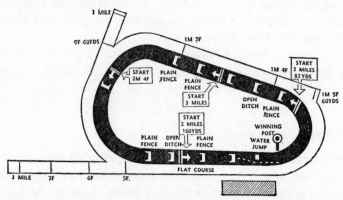

Although it stages no flat races of comparable stature to its valuable Schweppes Gold Trophy hurdle race or Hennessy Gold Cup steeplechase, both run here during the winter months, Newbury maintains a consistently high standard, and the proximity of the Berkshire and Wiltshire training centres ensures plenty of runners at most meetings. The left-handed oval track is about one mile seven furlongs round, galloping in nature and with easy bends. Trainers consider it a particularly good course for inexperienced two-year-olds, which accounts for the large fields commonplace for this type of event. In addition to the main course there is a straight mile, and another mile course which starts on a spur off the main circuit at the end of the back straight.

Principal races at Newbury include the Spring, Summer and Autumn Cups, which usually produce lively finishes; the Greenham Stakes (three-year-old colts) and Fred Darling Stakes (fillies) in April, which are among the most highly regarded of trials for the Guineas, and the Lockinge Stakes in September, an important prestige mile event.

The main grandstand has seen better days, but amenities are gradually being improved. The draw has no significant effect.

NEWCASTLE

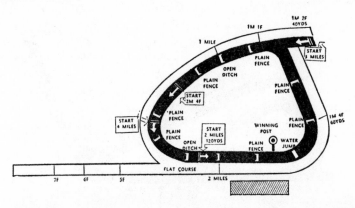

A bright, modern course in the attractive setting of Gosforth Park, just five miles from the centre of the city, Newcastle is deservedly popular with racegoers. For horses it is a stiff track, particularly when the going is heavy, and stamina and gameness are all-important. The last half mile of every race is uphill, so if you have any doubts about your horse getting the trip, keep your money in your pocket.

The track is a left-handed circuit of one and three-quarter miles, with a half-mile run-in. The turns are well banked, so they can be taken at speed, thus offering no chance of a 'breather' for a tiring horse. There is also a straight seven furlongs. The big race of the year is undoubtedly the two miles Northumberland Plate, in late June, first run in 1733, and an event which unfailingly draws a huge crowd. There is also a big handicap over one and a quarter miles in May, sponsored by Scottish and Newcastle Breweries.

Amenities are superb, the course having been virtually rebuilt in 1965, and the grandstands, which have escalators and gas-fired space heating, house betting halls, sparkling restaurants and bars. For children, there is an adventure playground which, it is claimed, is the most unusual on any course in Britain, as well as a more traditional type playground in the centre of the course.

The draw has no significant effect.

NEWMARKET

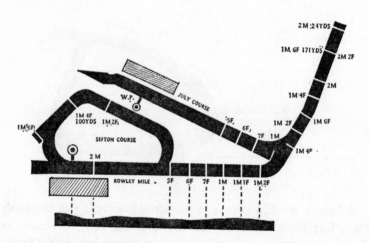

Newmarket is really two courses, which share a common starting point for their longer races and have separate run-ins. The main track is the Rowley Mile course which is, in fact, a perfectly straight one and a quarter miles over which most of the important events are contested. The pretty little July course is just a mile in length, also quite straight, and used, as its name implies, for the summer meetings only. It was on this track that the wartime Derbies and Guineas races were run. The bleak expanse of heath can be very forbidding at times, and for this reason, great and successful efforts have been made in recent years to improve spectators' comfort. An attractive balcony at the rear of the main grandstand overlooks the paddock and because the first half of long distance races on the traditional Rowley course are out of sight of the stands, a new right-handed circuit of nearly two miles round, the Sefton course, was opened in 1958.

There are many big races run at Newmarket, including the first two classics, the 2,000 Guineas and 1,000 Guineas in April; and at the two big October meetings the two legs of the 'Autumn Double', the Cambridgeshire, over nine furlongs, and the Cesarewitch, over two miles two furlongs as well as two important two-year-old events, the Middle Park Stakes and the Cheveley Park Stakes, both over six furlongs. Both the Cambridgeshire and Cesarewitch were first run in 1839, the latter being one of the races which is out of sight from the grandstand until it is half over. Because of this, it was once described as 'hanging about in Suffolk to see a race that is run in Cambridgeshire'. Principal event on the July course is the July Stakes, the oldest event in the calendar for two-year-olds.

Provided he is sufficiently stout-hearted not to be upset by the wide expanse before him, any horse should be capable of running well at Newmarket, and the excellent drainage means there are rarely any problems with the going. The draw has no significant effect on either of the Newmarket courses.

NOTTINGHAM

There was racing at Nottingham in the eighteenth century, but the present course, in Colwick Park, dates from 1892. An attractive course, it stages no particularly high-class events, but a growing number of sponsored races are helping to raise the standard. One of the executive's bright ideas is a minibus service to take spectators to the start if they wish to see this aspect of racing in close-up.

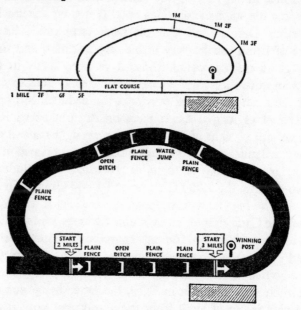

The track is a left-handed circuit of one and a half miles, with fairly easy turns and a run-in of four and a half furlongs. There is also a straight six furlongs. Nottingham tends to favour the sharp, well-balanced type of horse. The draw favours high numbers in sprints, and there is a slight advantage for low numbers on the round course. Principal race of the season is the Nottingham Stewards Cup, a six-furlong event that often attracts horses that have also run in the Goodwood equivalent.

PONTEFRACT

The Yorkshire town of Pontefract enjoyed its racing even in the troubled times of the English Civil War—in fact there was a meeting in progress while Cromwell's forces were laying siege to the castle in 1648, during one of the last campaigns of the war. Today, things tend to be less exciting and the course is one of the North's minor meetings.

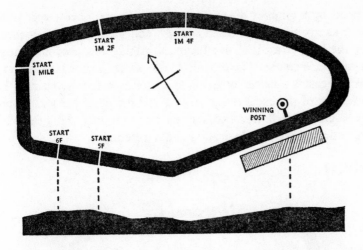

The track is left-handed, and one and a half miles round, with a sharp bend into the run-in of two furlongs. Although undulating in character, it presents a stern test of stamina, for the whole of the last three furlongs is uphill. As with Leicester, this is an important point to take into account when considering two-year-old races. Low numbers are best in the draw, especially in sprint races.

REDCAR

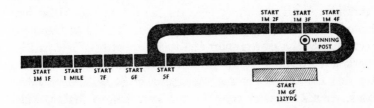

Racing used to take place on the sands at Redcar, and the bracing sea air still helps to make meetings at the attractive North Yorkshire course something special. Sponsored races, including one for women riders, are a feature of the programme, whose standard has risen spectacularly since the war.

The track is a long, narrow oval, almost two miles round,

joined by a straight nine furlongs. The bends, once considered very sharp, have been eased slightly, and their effect is lessened by the long straight of five furlongs, making this predominantly a galloper's course. The draw has little effect. A showpiece stand, which cost a quarter of a million pounds a few years ago, is a feature of the excellent amenities, and the paddocks and lawns have colourful flower beds which help towards the generally gay atmosphere of a basically holiday meeting.

RIPON

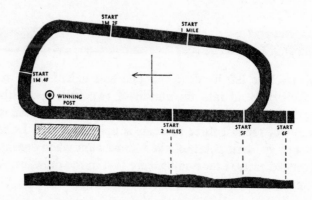

The town of Ripon has been associated with horses since at least Elizabethan times, and many of the big races staged at the Yorkshire course, midway between Harrogate and York, have historical links. Among them is the Great St Wilfrid Handicap, named after the patron saint of Ripon, whose feast day in 1837 marked the opening of the present course. Included in the prize for this £5,000 race is a silver trophy of St Wilfrid on horse-back. Another famous race is the Ripon Rowels Stakes, which acknowledges the fame the town enjoyed in past centuries for the spurs which were made here.

The track is right-handed, one mile five furlongs round, with a five-furlong run-in, and a six furlong straight course starting on a spur from it. It is undulating, and suits the handy type of horse best. Low numbers are best in the draw for races over five and six furlongs; high numbers on the round course.

SALISBURY

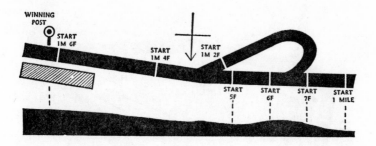

The thick covering of springy downland turf and the fair nature of the course make Salisbury a popular fixture with trainers, and a significantly high proportion of high-class two-year-olds make their racecourse debuts here. Brigadier Gerard won at Salisbury as an 'unknown' two-year-old, and just two hundred years earlier one of the all-time great names in racing, the legendary Eclipse, won the City Bowl, a race that is still run today. Salisbury has other links with the past. The Bibury Club, which has its home here, is the oldest race club in the country, dating back to 1681, although it only moved to Salisbury when the Stockbridge course was closed down in 1899. Queen Elizabeth I is reputed to have attended a Salisbury race meeting shortly before Drake sailed to defeat the Spanish Armada in 1588. The main prize then was a golden bell valued at £50 and won by the third Lord Cumberland.

The track today consists of a straight mile, with a right-handed loop at one end. Races of one and a half miles or more start in the straight, with the horses taking a left-hand turn into the loop and back into the straight again. Both stamina and adaptability are required of a horse running here for the track is undulating and the turn on the loop fairly sharp, while the last half mile of the straight is mostly uphill. High numbers are favoured by the draw on the straight course.

SANDOWN PARK

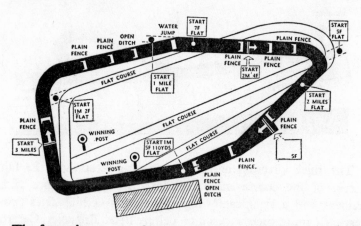

The favourite course of many racegoers, including at least one of the writers of this book, Sandown is situated in a natural amphitheatre and affords a perfect view of any race without recourse to the magnificent new grandstand, completed in 1973. Situated at Esher, just fifteen miles from London, Sandown was the first 'park' course, completely enclosed, to be built in Britain. The first meeting, in 1875, was a mixed jumping and flat race programme, and the April fixture today, in which a high-class flat-racing card is made even more attractive by the addition of the Whitbread Gold Trophy steeplechase, ranks as one of the finest single days' racing in the calendar. The most important race on the course, however, is the one and a quarter mile Eclipse Stakes in June, which regularly brings into opposition top classic horses of different generations. The 1886 Eclipse, incidentally, won by Bendigo, was the first £10,000 race ever to be run in Britain. The National Stakes, formerly known as the National Breeders Produce Stakes, used to be a major event in the two-year-old calendar and numbers the Aga Khan's undefeated Bahram among its winners, but has declined in importance in recent years.

The track is right-handed, and one mile five furlongs round, with a run-in of four furlongs which is all uphill. There is a separate five-furlongs course across the centre of the track, again entirely uphill, and Sandown is no place for the faint-hearted horse, although for the resolute type it is among the fairest in the land. The draw favours low numbers on the five-furlong course.

TEESSIDE PARK

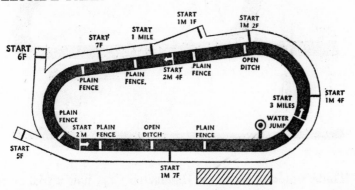

Flat racing returned to Teesside Park in 1974 after a couple of years of National Hunt meetings only. The course is close to Stockton-on-Tees, and was, in fact, called Stockton until 1966. The track is a left-handed oval of about one mile five furlongs with a run-in of four furlongs. The five-furlong track bends sharply left to join the main circuit at the entrance to the straight and there are other spurs for the six-furlong and nine-furlong starts.

Definitely a course for the sharp, nippy speed merchant, and certainly no place for the plodder. The draw gives a strong advantage to the low numbers.

THIRSK

New grandstands on the course and in the silver ring have helped increase the attractiveness of this popular Yorkshire meeting. The left-handed track is sharp in character, and only one and a quarter miles round, with easy turns. There is a straight six furlongs, not really suitable for the long-striding or awkward galloper, a factor that may account for the strange results that

M

frequently occur here. High numbers are best in the draw on the straight course.

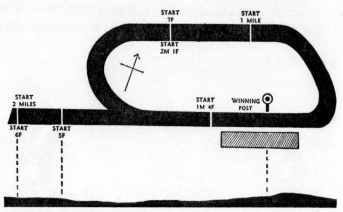

Thirsk's oldest race is the Hambleton Cup, now a trial event for the Cesarewitch, and in existence before the present course was opened in 1855. The most important nowadays, however, is the Thirsk Classic Trial in April, founded in 1948 when it was won by Alycidon, and since won by many subsequent classic winners, including Nimbus and Sweet Solera.

WARWICK

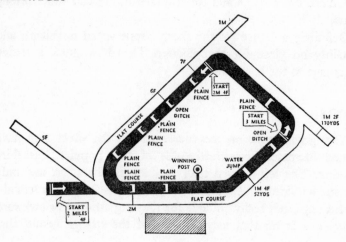

Noted nowadays more for its jumping meetings than the flat, Warwick stages average fare in pleasant enough surroundings through the summer months. It is a left-handed circuit of one and three-quarter miles, with a run-in of two and a half furlongs. The five-furlong course has a pronounced elbow just before it joins the main track for the run-in, hence the big advantage held by low numbers in the draw in races over this distance.

WINDSOR

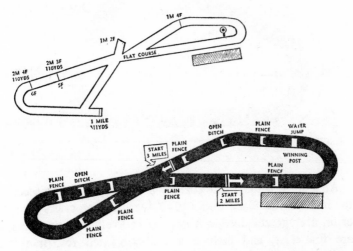

Close to the M4 motorway, and within easy reach of London, Windsor makes a speciality of midweek evening racing. The programme is usually of no more than moderate standard, but big fields are often attracted by events designed with this end in mind, so there is generally a good betting market to keep the customers reasonably happy. The unusual, figure-of-eight track, bounded on three sides by the River Thames, is just over one and three-quarter miles round, and although flat, has sharp bends. It provides plenty of problems for jockeys, and a competent rider is the first essential for any horse running here. The paddock, with its lime trees, is an attractive one, but the amenities generally are sub-standard, and the going can get very heavy in wet weather. High numbers are favoured by the draw in sprint races, but horses must start quickly to avoid being cut off at the elbow, just under half a mile from the post.

WOLVERHAMPTON

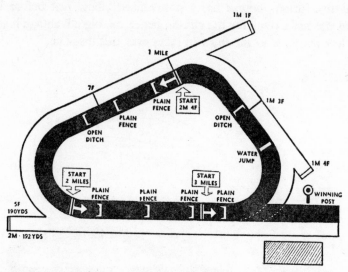

An enterprisingly run course, providing a pleasant oasis in the heart of the Black Country, Wolverhampton caters for racing of an average standard, but does so in lively fashion. Amenities are first-class, and include a well-appointed restaurant from which racing can be watched in comfort.

The oval track is left-handed, one mile five furlongs round, and almost entirely flat, with easy turns and a run-in of five furlongs, which makes it ideal for the long-striding galloper. There is a straight course of five furlongs one hundred and ninety yards, on which the draw is considered to favour high numbers.

Wolverhampton's feature races include its own version of the big Newmarket autumn double, the Midlands Cambridgeshire and Midlands Cesarewitch, both run in September–October.

YARMOUTH

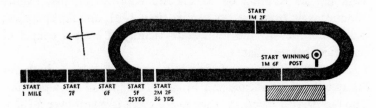

A modest little corporation-owned course, sometimes referred to as 'Newmarket by the Sea' because of the habit of stables from the town, seventy miles away, 'farming' the races here. The grandstand faces the sea, and is apt to become uncomfortably crowded on sunny days when there is a big crowd of holiday-makers.

The track is left-handed, one and a quarter miles round, and generally easy, although the five-furlongs run-in can find out short-runners, which accounts for some of the form upsets for which the track is famous. There is a straight mile, level all the way. The course is laid out on what were formerly sand dunes, and the sandy sub-soil means the track possesses excellent drainage qualities, with the result that heavy going is practically unheard of. The draw is said to favour high numbers in races on the straight course, but the effect is only very marginal.

YORK

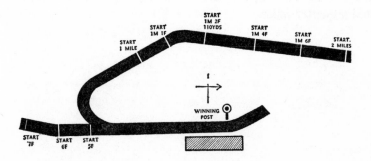

Always the principal racing centre in the North of England, York has seen racing on its historic Knavesmire, just twenty minutes' walk from the city centre, since 1731, and the sport was well established in the immediate vicinity at least a couple of centuries before that.

Today, York is one of Britain's great racecourses, both for the quality of its racing and in the excellence of its amenities. The big August meeting, when every event is worth over £1,000 to the winner, fully deserves its description as the Royal Ascot of the North.

The three-sided track is two miles long and perfectly level, with long, sweeping turns and a five-furlongs run-in. It is a very fair test of the thoroughbred. There is also a seven-furlongs straight course joining the main track at the turn into the straight. The draw has no significance at York.

The oldest of the big races staged at York is the one and three-quarter miles Ebor Handicap, which always provides the highlight of the Wednesday card at the August festival. It was first run in 1845, and at that time was the only event of less than four miles run at the meeting! Other famous races at the festival include the Gimcrack Stakes for two-year-olds, named after the famous grey who won twenty-seven of his thirty-five races; the five-furlong Nunthorpe Stakes, in which two-year-olds are permitted to take on their elders; and the Great Voltigeur Stakes over one and a half miles, a trial for the St Leger. The three-day May meeting features the Yorkshire Cup (one and three-quarter miles) and two highly regarded classic trials, the Dante Stakes and the Musidora Stakes, the latter for fillies only, both run over one and a quarter miles.

Fig 6 Locations of racecourses in Ireland

Irish Courses

THE CURRAGH

Ireland's principal flat racing course, thirty miles south-west of Dublin, The Curragh is the setting for all the Irish classic races, the most important of which is without doubt the Irish Sweeps Derby, now established as one of the great races of Europe. Run each July, this one and a half miles contest for three-year-olds often brings into opposition the Derby winners of England and France, as well as many other top-class horses. Surprise results are not uncommon. Both Sir Ivor and Roberto were beaten here after winning at Epsom.

The Curragh is situated in County Kildare, and the amenities include a nursery where children may be safely left while parents enjoy the racing. The course is right-handed, and fairly stiff, with an uphill finish. The draw has no significant effect.

Big races, apart from the Irish Sweeps Derby, are the Irish Guiness Oaks, and the Irish 2,000 and 1,000 Guineas in May.

LEOPARDSTOWN

Known primarily as a jumping course (it is the home of the valuable Irish Sweeps Hurdle), Leopardstown also stages flat racing in the summer, and its wide finishing straight has a movable running rail to enable the best ground to be used for racing. The track is left-handed, and eminently suitable for galloping types. The course itself is the most modern in Ireland, having been almost completely rebuilt in 1970 with a new luxury stand. It is situated near Dun Laoghaire (Kingstown) about ten miles from Dublin.

Big races include the Player-Wills Stakes and the Hennessy Handicap. The draw has little significance, although low numbers are thought to hold a very slight advantage in races over seven furlongs and a mile.

OTHER COURSES

Of Ireland's other courses, only one, Laytown, in County Meath, is exclusively for flat racing. The rest all stage both National Hunt and flat races, although the latter are often simply, 'introductory' events for potential hurdlers and steeplechasers.

Appendices

I Directory of Organisations in Racing

OFFICIAL ORGANISATIONS

The Jockey Club (all communications to The Secretary) 42 Portman Square, London, W1. Tel: 01–486 4921. *Horserace Betting Levy Board*, 17–23 Southampton Row, London, WC1. Tel: 01–405 5346. *Racing Information Bureau*, 42 Portman Square, London, W1. Tel: 01–486 4571. *Tattersall's Committee*, 7–9 Hatherley Road, Reading, Berks. Tel: Reading 65402. *Racecourse Association*, 42 Portman Square, London, W1. Tel: 01–486 3082. *Horserace Totalisator Board*, 163 Euston Road, London, NW1. Tel: 01–387 3140. *Racecourse Technical Services Ltd*, 88 Bushey Road, Raynes Park, London, SW20. Tel: 01–947 3333. *International Racing Bureau* (Secretary: David Hedges), 154 Brompton Road, London, SW3. Tel: 01–584 9642.

PROFESSIONAL ORGANISATIONS

The National Trainers Association, 5 Stone Buildings, Lincolns Inn, London, WC2. Tel: 01–242 4136. *The Jockeys Association of Great Britain* (Secretary: Peter Smith), 16 The Broadway, Newbury, Berks. Tel: Newbury 4102. *The Racehorse Owners Association* (Secretary: Don Cox), 42 Portman Square, London, W1. Tel: 01–486 6977. *National Association of Bookmakers*, Sabian House, 26–27 Cowcross Street, London, EC1. Tel: 01–253 0044. *National Sporting League* (Bookmakers), 148

Temple Chambers, Temple Avenue, London, EC4. Tel: 01–583 0071. *The Thoroughbred Breeders' Association,* 28 Bloomsbury Way, London, WC1. Tel: 01–405 4777. *British Veterinary Association,* 7 Mansfield Street, Portland Place, London, W1. Tel: 01–636 6541. *Animal Health Trust,* 14 Ashley Place, London, SW1. Tel: 01–834 3207. *(Equine Research Station)* Balaton Lodge, Newmarket, Suffolk. Tel: Newmarket 2241. *The Horserace Writers Association* (Clerk: Elizabeth Hearn), 4 Preston Hill, Kenton, Middlesex. Tel: 01–204 3175. *The Bloodstock Breeders and Horse Owners' Association of Ireland,* 9 Merrion Square, Dublin, 2. Tel: Dublin 66842.

GENERAL

The Racegoers Club (Secretary: A. M. Fairbairn), 42 Portman Square, London, W1. Tel: 01–486 4571. *Daily Mirror Punters Club, c/o Daily Mirror,* High Holborn, London, EC4. Tel: 01–353 0246. *John Banks Sporting Club International* (Racecard analysis, special information etc), Moores Chambers, Charters Road, Sunningdale, Ascot, Berks. Tel: Ascot 24854. *Ayres and Newbon Ltd* (Racing publicity), 29 Woodway, Plymstock, Plymouth, Devon. Tel: Plymouth 44481.

FORM SERVICES

Raceform Ltd (Official weekly formbook, private handicap ratings thrice weekly, daily telephone service), Raceform House, 29–31 York Road, London, SW11. Tel: 01–223 1183. *Timeform Ltd* (Annual, *Racehorses of 19 . .,* detailing every horse that ran in previous season; weekly formbook; race ratings thrice weekly and special racecards for every meeting with detailed form summaries and ratings for every runner; daily telephone service), Timeform House, Northgate, Halifax, Yorks.

NEWSPAPERS AND PERIODICALS

Sporting Chronicle (daily). *Sporting Life* (daily). *Racing*

Calendar (weekly), available on subscription only from Messrs Weatherby, Sanders Road, Wellingborough, Northants. *Sporting Chronicle Handicap Book*, contains details of coming week's programmes (weekly, Fridays). *Horse and Hound* (weekly, Fridays). *The Racehorse* (weekly, Fridays). *Racing & Football Outlook* (weekly, Tuesdays). *The Winner* (weekly, Wednesdays). *Irish Racingform* (weekly). *Stud & Stable* (monthly). *Pacemaker and Racing Ahead* (monthly). *The British Racehorse* (quarterly). *The Licensed Bookmaker and Betting Office Proprietor* (monthly).

II Official Scale of Weight-for-Age

Distance	Age	MAR-APR	MAY	JUNE	JULY	AUG	SEPT	OCT	NOV
		st lb	st lb	st lb	st lb	st lb	st lb	st lb	st lb
5f	2	5 11	6 2	6 7	6 10	7 2	7 6	7 10	7 12
	3	8 1	8 3	8 5	8 7	8 9	8 11	8 13	8 13
	4	9 0	9 0	9 0	9 0	9 0	9 0	9 0	9 0
	5	9 0	9 0	9 0	9 0	9 0	9 0	9 0	9 0
6f	2	—	5 13	6 2	6 6	6 9	7 1	7 4	7 7
	3	7 13	8 1	8 3	8 5	8 7	8 9	8 11	8 11
	4	9 0	9 0	9 0	9 0	9 0	9 0	9 0	9 0
	5	9 0	9 0	9 0	9 0	9 0	9 0	9 0	9 0
7f	2	—	—	—	—	—	6 11	7 0	7 3
	3	7 11	7 13	8 1	8 3	8 5	8 7	8 9	8 10
	4	9 0	9 0	9 0	9 0	9 0	9 0	9 0	9 0
	5	9 0	9 0	9 0	9 0	9 0	9 0	9 0	9 0
1m	2	—	—	—	—	—	6 7	6 10	7 0
	3	7 10	7 12	8 0	8 2	8 4	8 6	8 8	8 10
	4	9 0	9 0	9 0	9 0	9 0	9 0	9 0	9 0
	5	9 0	9 0	9 0	9 0	9 0	9 0	9 0	9 0
9f	3	7 9	7 11	7 13	8 1	8 3	8 5	8 7	8 9
	4	9 0	9 0	9 0	9 0	9 0	9 0	9 0	9 0
	5	9 1	9 0	9 0	9 0	9 0	9 0	9 0	9 0
1¼m	3	7 8	7 10	7 12	8 0	8 2	8 4	8 6	8 8
	4	9 0	9 0	9 0	9 0	9 0	9 0	9 0	9 0
	5	9 2	9 1	9 0	9 0	9 0	9 0	9 0	9 0
11f	3	7 7	7 9	7 11	7 13	8 1	8 3	8 5	8 7
	4	9 0	9 0	9 0	9 0	9 0	9 0	9 0	9 0
	5	9 3	9 2	9 1	9 0	9 0	9 0	9 0	9 0
1½m	3	7 6	7 8	7 10	7 12	8 1	8 3	8 5	8 7
	4	9 0	9 0	9 0	9 0	9 0	9 0	9 0	9 0
	5	9 4	9 3	9 2	9 1	9 0	9 0	9 0	9 0
13f	3	7 5	7 7	7 9	7 11	8 0	8 2	8 4	8 6
	4	9 0	9 0	9 0	9 0	9 0	9 0	9 0	9 0
	5	9 5	9 4	9 3	9 2	9 0	9 0	9 0	9 0
1¾m	3	7 5	7 7	7 9	7 11	8 0	8 2	8 4	8 6
	4	9 0	9 0	9 0	9 0	9 0	9 0	9 0	9 0
	5	9 6	9 4	9 3	9 2	9 0	9 0	9 0	9 0
15f	3	7 4	7 6	7 8	7 10	7 13	8 1	8 3	8 5
	4	9 0	9 0	9 0	9 0	9 0	9 0	9 0	9 0
	5	9 6	9 4	9 3	9 2	9 0	9 0	9 0	9 0
2m	3	7 4	7 6	7 8	7 10	7 13	8 1	8 3	8 5
	4	9 0	9 0	9 0	9 0	9 0	9 0	9 0	9 0
	5	9 6	9 4	9 3	9 2	9 0	9 0	9 0	9 0
2¼m	3	7 3	7 5	7 7	7 9	7 12	8 0	8 2	8 4
	4	9 0	9 0	9 0	9 0	9 0	9 0	9 0	9 0
	5	9 7	9 5	9 4	9 3	9 2	9 0	9 0	9 0
2½m	3	7 2	7 4	7 6	7 8	7 11	7 13	8 1	8 3
	4	9 0	9 0	9 0	9 0	9 0	9 0	9 0	9 0
	5	9 7	9 5	9 4	9 3	9 2	9 0	9 0	9 0

III Racing Records
(Great Britain)

FASTEST TIMES: FIVE FURLONGS

	mins secs
INDIGENOUS, Epsom, June 2, 1960	0 53³/₅

SIX FURLONGS

BROKEN TINDRIL, Brighton, August 6, 1929	1 6³/₅

ONE MILE

SOUEIDA, Brighton, September 19, 1963	1 31⁴/₅
LOOSE COVER, Brighton, June 9, 1966	1 31⁴/₅

RECORD TIMES OF GREAT RACES

2,000 GUINEAS (1 mile), MY BABU, 1948	1 35⁴/₅
1,000 GUINEAS (1 mile), CAMAREE, 1950	1 37
DERBY (1 mile, 4 furlongs), MAHMOUD, 1936	2 33⁴/₅
OAKS (1 mile, 4 furlongs), BEAM, 1927	2 34³/₅
ST LEGER (1 mile, 6 furlongs, 132 yards), CORONACH 1926, and WINDSOR LAD, 1934	3 1³/₅

Richest 2,000 Guineas—1964, BALDIC II, £40,302 10s.
Richest 1,000 Guineas—1964, POURPARLER; £29,102 15s.
Richest Derby—1966, CHARLOTTOWN; £74,489 10s.
Richest St Leger—1964, INDIANA; £43,558.
Richest Oaks—1966, VALORIS; £35,711 10s.

Winnings of Famous Racehorses—BRIGADIER GERARD £253,023, MILL REEF £133,170 and £135,937, in France, NIJINSKY £238,715, BLAKENEY £63,108, SIR IVOR £97,076 and £37,000 in the United States, RIBOCCO £100,286, ROYAL PALACE £92,998, SODIUM £95,322, MEADOW COURT £87,158, SEA BIRD II £65,301, SANTA CLAUS £134,687 (inc £62,620 in Ireland), RAGUSA £114,744 (inc £49,152 10s in Ireland), BALLYMOSS £98,651 (inc £37,925 in France and £7,464 in Ireland), ST PADDY £97,193, RELKO £80,094 15s (inc £44,156 5s in France), TULYAR £76,417, PETITE ETOILE £67,785, ISLINGLASS £57,455, DONOVAN £55,154, ALCIDE £54,382, HULA DANCER £50,848.

Record price for a British thoroughbred at public auction is 136,000 guineas by A. YANK (World Wide B. A. of United States) for VAGUELY NOBLE, Newmarket Sales, December 1967.

Record price for a yearling is 117,000 guineas for a NATIVE PRINCE colt out of Review, paid by Curragh Bloodstock Agency, Newmarket Sales, October 16, 1971.

Record price for a foal at public auction is 37,000 guineas for a chestnut filly foal by Exbury—Loose Cover, paid by British Bloodstock Agency, Newmarket Sales, December 1968.

Record price for a horse in training is 136,000 guineas for VAGUELY NOBLE, December 1967, at the Newmarket Sales.

Record owner's winnings for one season—Mr CHARLES ENGELHARD, 1970, £182,056.

Record winning mounts for one season—G. RICHARDS, 1947, 269.

Record trainer's winnings for one season—N. MURLESS, 1967, £256,699.

Glossary of Racing Terms

Acceptor: Any horse left in a race after a set date, up to which owners have the option of withdrawing their entries. The term originated from handicaps in which, by leaving his horse in a race, an owner 'accepts' the handicapper's estimate of his chance.

Accumulator: A bet on four or more horses collectively. One loser and the whole stake is lost.

Added money: That part of a race's prize money which comes from the course or a sponsor, as distinct from the sums paid by owners.

Aged: A horse that is more than six years old.

Also ran: A runner that finishes out of the first three.

Amiss: A mare or filly found to be 'in season'—this is often the reason for an inexplicably poor display in a race.

Ante-post: Advance betting on big races—the punter gets better odds, in theory at any rate, than by waiting until the day of the race, but if the horse does not run he loses his stake.

Bar: A term used in betting displays, meaning 'the rest' or 'those not quoted'.

Baulked: When a horse is hampered by a rival running directly across his path.

Blinkers: Eye-shields, usually attached to a cloth hood, fitted to help a horse concentrate. Sometimes called 'blinds' by jockeys.

Blower: A telephone system by which bookmakers relay money from off-course bets to agents on the course.

Blow-up: When a horse which has been up with the leaders suddenly drops out and almost stops. Also known as 'dying'. Usually a sign of his being not quite 100 per cent fit.

Bumper: An amateur rider.

Bumping and boring: Term used to describe a horse knocking a rival off balance. Usually followed by an objection or stewards' inquiry.

Came again: Renewed his challenge.

Cast in his box: A horse which has gone down in his horsebox or stable and has difficulty in getting up again.

Chalk Jockey: A rider who has not yet ridden often enough at the course to have a painted nameboard in the runners and riders frame. His name will, therefore, be written up in chalk.

Colt: A male horse under five years of age.

Distance: The official winning margin when one runner comes home streets ahead of all its rivals.

Divots: Lumps of turf scooped out by horses' hooves.

Dog: A horse that obviously dislikes racing. Also sometimes called a 'leary'.

Dolls: Hurdles placed across part of a course as direction markers.

Double: A bet on two horses, both of which must win (or be placed in the case of a place double) for the wager to be successful. An each-way double is two separate doubles: one to win, the other for a place.

N

Dwell: To be slow out of the stalls or away from the starting gate.

Dying: See 'Blow-up'.

Each way: Backing a horse to win and to be placed in the first two or three, according to the number of runners.

Entire: A male horse that has not been gelded.

Extravagant: Description of a horse that moves with great freedom.

Filly: A female horse under five years of age.

Forecast: Tote bet in which you have to name the first two horses, in correct order or either order according to the number of runners.

Form: A horse's ability as shown by his running in previous races.

Free handicap: An 'invitation' race for which owners pay no fee until the acceptance stage.

Front runner: A horse that likes to lead all the way.

Gelding: A castrated horse.

Genuine: Description of a horse that is always trying his best.

Gibbing: A horse refusing to obey his rider's commands.

Greenness: Inexperience.

Hack: To ride gently.

Hand: Unit of length (four inches) used to measure the size of a horse, taken from the ground to the horse's withers. Most horses are around sixteen hands high.

Hang: To veer strongly to one side.

Head: See Length.

Hood: See Blinkers.

In the frame: Placed in the first four. The expression comes from the fact that the result of each race is shown on the course by the numbers of the first four horses being placed in a frame on the runners board.

Irons: Stirrups.

Jackpot: Tote pool for which you have to name six consecutive winners.

Leary: See 'Dog'.

Leathers: Stirrup straps.

Leg: The expression 'has a leg' usually refers to a horse suffering from a sprained tendon.

Length: Measurement of distance between horses during, or at the finish of, a race. About 8ft—the length of an average horse from nose to tail. Shorter official winning margins (in order of closeness) are short-head, head, neck, half a length and three-quarters of a length.

Maiden: A horse that has never won.

Mare: A female horse aged five or over.

Match: A race between two horses on terms agreed between their respective owners. It was with such contests that racing began.

Neck: See Length.

Objection: Official complaint by trainer, owner or jockey of one runner against another in the race. It must be made in writing and accompanied by a deposit of £5.00 which is forfeited if the stewards consider there were not reasonable grounds for the objection. If they consider it frivolous, they can impose an additional fine of up to £20.

Outsider: A runner quoted in the betting at long odds against.

Over the top: Said of a horse that is past his fitness peak.

Overweight: The amount by which the weight of the jockey, plus his equipment, exceeds that which the horse is set to carry.

Photo-finish: When the judge calls for the evidence of the camera to determine or confirm his placings. Denoted by a letter 'P' in the results frame.

Plate: A race whose prize money is fixed at an advertised value. Also term given to the light steel or aluminium shoes worn by horses for racing.

Plodder: A one-paced horse.

Pressure: A jockey riding all out.

Puller: A horse that constantly fights for his head.

Punter: Slang term for anyone who bets on horse racing.

Put down: To end the life of a (usually badly injured) horse.

Rails: Inside boundary fence of the course.

Returns (or SP returns): Starting price details.

Ride work: To take part in training gallops.

Rig: A male horse whose testicles have not properly developed.

Ringer: A horse substituted for another with intent to defraud.

Rogue: A horse that refuses to do his best.

Roll-up: Special Tote bet in which punters were required to forecast the first six horses in a selected race in the correct finishing order.

Running on: A horse lengthening his stride at the end of a race.

Scratched: A horse taken out of a race for which he has been entered is said to have been 'scratched'.

Shoes: A horse's usual footwear for ordinary roadwork. Made of steel and much heavier than the plates worn for racing.

Short head: The minimum official winning distance. *See* Length.

Show: A list of runners with their latest betting odds.

Shy: When a horse veers away suddenly from an object, real or imaginary.

Stayer: A horse capable of racing over long distances.

Sweepstake: A race in which all entry fees, forfeits etc, go to the winner or placed horses.

Treble: A bet similar to a double, but on three horses instead of two.

Unsound: A term applied to a horse that has a physical defect.

Upsides: Alongside.

Walk-over: A race with only one runner. The jockey is required to weigh out, mount at the correct time, and canter past the stands. The owner collects second and third prize money as well as that for the winner.

Whip round: To turn about suddenly at the start. The cause of many horses being left at the old-style starting gate.

Yankee: A combination bet in which the punter backs four horses in eleven different ways (six doubles, four trebles and one four-horse accumulator).

Acknowledgements

The authors would like to thank all the many people who gave so much of their time to provide invaluable help with the preparation of this book and the checking of the manuscript and proofs.

In particular, we are indebted to David Hedges, director of the International Racing Bureau, for his assistance in compiling the foreign racing chapter; and Duncan Keith for his expert help with the chapter on jockeys.

Others to whom we extend our grateful thanks include David and Jennifer Barons; Willie Carson; Don Cox, of the Racehorse Owners' Association; Major Peter Edes and Brigadier Sam Weller, of the Racecourse Association; Tony Fairbairn, Louise Gold and Ron Hammond, of the Racing Information Bureau; Raleigh Gilbert, Dorothy Laird, John Meyer, of Racecourse Technical Services; Carl Nekola; Fulke Walwyn; Billy Williams, and the staff of Messrs Weatherby.

Our thanks are also due to Alison Beer for carrying out the arduous work of typing the manuscripts, and last, but certainly not least, to Maggie and Katie, for coping so valiantly with all the headaches, heartaches, and burnt suppers that are the inevitable consequence of marriage to a writer!

Index

Numerals in bold face refer to illustrations